IF
LOVE
COULD
THINK

IF
LOVE
COULD
THINK

USING YOUR MIND TO GUIDE
YOUR HEART

ALON GRATCH, Ph.D.

HARMONY BOOKS
NEW YORK

HARMONY BOOKS is a registered trademark and the Harmony Books
colophon is a trademark of Random House, Inc.

Library of Congress Cataloging-in-Publication Data

Gratch, Alon.
If love could think : using your mind to guide your heart / Alon Gratch.—1st
ed.
Includes bibliographical references.
1. Man-woman relationships—Psychological aspects. 2. Love.
3. Ambivalence. I. Title.
HQ801.G665   2005
646.7'7—dc22   2005013622
1-4000-9815-7

Printed in the United States of America

Design by Lauren Dong

10 9 8 7 6 5 4 3 2 1

First Editon

To Ilana, Jordan, and Michele,
who taught me so much about love

Author's Note

All the cases described in this book are composites. They have been deliberately mixed and altered in order to protect my patients' rights of confidentiality and privacy. No patient found in this book corresponds to any actual person, living or dead.

ACKNOWLEDGMENTS

First and foremost, I'd like to thank my patients, past and present, from whose struggles, successes, and failures I've learned both professionally and personally. It would be impossible to mention by name all the other people—friends, lovers, colleagues, supervisors, and supervisees—who, in crossing my path over the years, have contributed to my development as a psychologist and an author. Indirectly, they have all influenced the ideas presented in this book.

More directly, I'm greatly indebted to a few individuals who have either shaped my thinking about love or encouraged and supported my desire to write about it. My wife and colleague, Michele Sacks, is simply the best. My analyst, Betty Hellman, and my colleagues/ friends Brenda Berger and Ivan Bresgi have all been great sounding boards and generous supporters.

I would also like to express my deep gratitude to my agent, Tracy Brown, whose wise counsel, experience, and support have been invaluable, and to Kim Meisner, my editor at Harmony Books, who brought to the project tremendous enthusiasm, intelligence, and clarity; and to the following individuals for their kind and professional handling of me and the manuscript: Dorthe Binkert of Scherz Verlag, Christophe Guias of Editions Payot, Paul Christophe of Editora Campus, and Thanos Grammenos of Thymari.

Last but not least, I'd like to thank my parents, Haya and Avraham Gratch, and my brothers, Eliezer Gadot and Ariel Gratch, and their families for their continued interest and support.

CONTENTS

3

One Way Love   90

4

Triangular Love   118

5

Forbidden Love *151*

6

Sexual Love *173*

7

Androgynous Love *202*

IF
LOVE
COULD
THINK

When Love Goes Wrong

*Everything in life is metamorphosis, in plants and in
animals, up to and including mankind as well.*
GOETHE

"When love goes wrong, nothing goes right." So goes
the song and so say my psychotherapy patients,
if not in words, then in symptoms and disorders.
When love goes wrong, our soul goes wrong—and our minds
play tricks on us. Depression, anxiety, panic attacks, sexual problems, stress, alcoholism, and drug addiction are all disturbances
in our dialogue with love. As simplistic as it may sound, our fail-
ings in love are at the theoretical core of the most sophisticated
schools of developmental psychology. Which is why I set out to
learn and teach—and now write—about the sixty-four-million-
dollar question of why love goes wrong and what, if anything,
can make it right.

The patterns of failed love are by now a cliché familiar to us
all. Yet the underlying problem and what to do about it still baf-
fle us. This book is for anyone struggling with these patterns.
Whether you're contemplating breaking up a relationship or
whether you already broke it off and don't want to repeat the
same pattern in the next relationship, whether you are dating
endlessly without being able to find the right person or whether

you find yourself once again in a long-term relationship with the wrong person, whether you're wondering if you should go ahead with the wedding plans or whether you're questioning if you're stuck in a loveless marriage, or if you're simply fascinated by the mysteries of love and want to witness and decipher the dramatic and moving journeys of some of its most adventurous explorers—my patients—this book is for you.

Over the years, while helping my patients to wrestle with the problem of love, I've come to see that relationship patterns are not simply a repetition of a single, distinct behavior. For example, if your pattern is about getting involved with unavailable men, it is unlikely that all of them have been unavailable in the same way. One of your relationships may have been a long-distance one, another, with a man who couldn't commit, and a third with a man who was married or secretly bisexual. Furthermore, if this is your pattern, it is also likely that in order to overcome it, you have tried, probably more than once, to date someone *you* were not really attracted to but who was very much interested in you. In other words, your pattern included being on the other side of the equation.

This overlapping, interrelated nature of relationship patterns, we shall soon see, is not merely an incidental characteristic of our messy interpersonal landscape. It's to a large extent a consequence of the fact that these romantic patterns have a common psychological ancestor, one that we must understand if we are to attain love. Though it feels like it should be pure, love can never be so, because neither its giver nor its receiver are. Where there is love, there is always hate, or to put it in more palatable language, there's always anger and disappointment—precisely because we care so much. To love requires that we be vulnerable, but being vulnerable makes us hate—hate the person who "makes" us feel that way. That's why we say we "fall in love," not "stand in love," and that's why so much music, poetry, literature, and movies are a variation on the theme of "Falling in love again, never wanted to, what am I to do, can't help it."

In his book *Can Love Last?* psychologist Stephen Mitchell captured the essence of this ambivalence. Drawing on a metaphor used by Nietzsche to demonstrate man's struggle with his mortality, Mitchell describes romantic love as akin to building a sand castle on the beach. We must invest all our passion into it while at the same time keep in mind that at any moment it can all be washed away by the tide. This, of course, is a difficult state of mind to maintain, and as Mitchell put it, in order to manage it we "split" our exciting but uncertain sand castle into "stone castles" and "castles in the sky." The former are our stable yet boring long-term relationships or marriages, and the latter are our fantasies or brief encounters of romantic ecstasy and sexual novelty. While neither makes us happy, in both cases we are safe from the uncertainty, risk, and vulnerability inherent in love. In the "stone castles" we might have too much reality and not enough fantasy, but at least we feel safe in their predictability and strength. In the "castles in the sky" we may have too much fantasy and not enough reality, but then again we don't have much to lose—other than our illusions. As I will demonstrate throughout this book, the patterns of failed love are all based on this split. In trying to avoid the reality of love—its inherently ambivalent nature—we escape into ultimately untenable fantasies of perfect love.

A BRIEF HISTORY OF AMBIVALENCE (THE WAR OF THE BREASTS)

One of the biggest controversies in the history of psychoanalysis is whether this ambivalence in our relation to love originates in a three- or a two-person psychology. In Freudian theory, the problem begins when a third party, the father, is introduced into the relatively harmonious picture of the mother-child relationship. When the father enters the child's interpersonal world—at least historically a couple of years after the mother—the child begins to compete with the same-sex parent for the love of the opposite-sex parent. In this Oedipal drama, the child is afraid of retaliation from his competitor and can't help but develop resentments toward both parents for putting him in this predicament. Hence, love and hate are interwoven.

In more contemporary theories, the trouble with love is thought to start much earlier, in the presumed bliss of the mother-child duo. Cognitively and emotionally, these theories go, the infant is unable to accept that the mother who feeds and cares for him is the same creature who sometimes deprives him. In his mind, the infant therefore splits the mother into two—in symbolic psychoanalytic terms, "the good breast" and the "bad breast." Emotionally, this is necessary so that the infant's rage toward the imperfect, depriving mother will not destroy his love for the idealized all-giving mother. In other words, the ambivalence toward the love object is there from the very beginning, but it's so threatening to the infant that he must deny it.

At present, most psychoanalytic theorists agree that we don't need to get rid of Freud altogether in order to accept the primary importance of the early mother-child relationship. Indeed, Oedipal and pre-Oedipal theories complement each other only too well, and together they provide a powerful developmental explanation as to the problem with love. We start life with a fundamental ambivalence toward the object of our dependency—usually the mother—who can never be perfect, and when the second parent enters our consciousness, the unavoidable competition only deepens our ambivalence. And of course, there are also siblings and other creatures whom we love and need but who we also wish would disappear from our emotional radar.

And to top it all, there are the inevitable losses, disappointments, and hurts that start as soon as the child ventures out of the family home and that continue throughout life—cementing and reinforcing our ambivalent, love-hate relationship.

Now, think about your own relationships with your parents in childhood. Did you feel they loved you? Probably. Did you love them? Most likely. But did you also feel judged, disappointed, or even betrayed by them? And did you also feel angry with or happy to get away from them? Did you feel you didn't get enough from one of your parents or perhaps too much from the other? If you answer "never" to each of last three questions you might well be like those patients of mine who in the initial consultation defensively exclaim that theirs were the most wonderful parents in the world, to which I respond with an internal sigh that I have my work cut out for me. The point is, our early and inherently ambivalent relationships with our parents—inherently ambivalent because being a parent is an impossible job—literally leaves an imprint on our developing young brain, which we subsequently can't help but "superimpose" on our adult relationships.

So yes, ambivalence is not only here to stay, but it's also an integral part of the human condition. And yet, we are so frightened by it that we often choose an illusion of pure love over its more multifaceted reality. When I mention the concept of ambivalence to patients, they always want to know more. They intuitively understand its importance and they are intrigued. But they often confuse *ambivalent* with *ambiguous,* which means vague or unclear—perhaps because they are so afraid of their ambivalence that they welcome a certain amount of ambiguity in their thinking about it. They need not fear, however, because the problem with love is not ambivalence itself but rather how we deal, or don't deal, with it. So yes, there is an alternative to illusional love. By changing the way we think about love or simply by *thinking* when we are in love, we can learn to manage rather than to deny our ambivalence.

METAMORPHOSIZING LOVE

As always in psychology, at least conceptually, the solution is simpler than the problem. The complexity of the problem—the patterns of failed love in our case—obscures the simplicity of the solution. When you think about it, ambivalence is only a problem when we approach love with the idea that we're supposed to *get* something out of it. For example, I may not be willing to commit to my girlfriend if I think that she is not smart enough—because I will not be able to have stimulating conversations with her. Or if she is not attractive enough, I will be less aroused by her and sex won't be as good. Or if my boyfriend is not communicative enough, my feelings will not be validated. Or if he works too much, he will not be there for me. Or if he doesn't make a lot of money, I will not have the kind of lifestyle I'm accustomed to. Or if he hates traveling, I will never be able to go to Europe on vacation.

Obviously, in this approach to love—which is probably the primary one in our culture—the important thing is *what I expect to receive* from my partner. Of course, depending on the degree of my emotional hunger, no partner may ever have enough to fill me up. Nonetheless, by definition, in this model, our capacity for love depends on the other person: Whether we attribute it to "karma" or to psychology, we expect to fall in love when the "right person" comes along. And we expect that to happen even though it flies in the face of everything we know about love: (1) we fall in love with the wrong people all the time, and (2) those who wait for the "one and only," or the "truly" right person, end up on life's waiting list.

The truth is that the capacity for love depends not on the other person but on ourselves, because love is primarily about giving, not receiving. In romantic relationships, however, this definition of love seems like a tall order. "What about *my* needs?" is what most of us ask our lover, and "What am *I* getting out of this relationship?" is what we ask ourselves. But strangely, in other kinds of love relationships, it's pretty easy to attain. Parents, for example, don't stop loving their children because they are not smart enough or pretty enough or because they are boring or act out. Unlike with a lover, they don't just leave their child because they "lost interest" or "outgrew" him or "fell out of love."

Now, in the case of parents, it's our job, our responsibility, to love. Giving is the expressed purpose of this relationship and therefore, at least consciously, we don't expect anything in return. Which is precisely why the good-enough parent doesn't have much trouble feeling love for his child, no matter how ambivalent he or she feels about the child's imperfections. But the idea of love not expecting anything in return is much deeper, of course, than a job or duty. It is likely hardwired within us, for our survival in the evolution of the species has always rested on our ability to care for offspring who—unlike those of any other species—were utterly helpless and completely dependent on their parents for a long time after birth.

Whether or not we are parents ourselves, deep within us we all have the capacity to give, and in fact when we first fall in love it all comes back to us in the form of happy and unconditional generosity. But soon enough we begin to think about *our* needs and lose touch with the idea of not expecting anything in return. Why is that? And why can't we later on switch back to this earlier notion of love? Why can't we redefine love—*it's about giving, not receiving, stupid!*? The reason, I believe, is that many of us seek in adult relationships the kind of love we didn't receive enough of in our childhood. In a sense, we feel emotionally deprived, and unless it's our role or duty to love, we feel as though we have nothing to give and we revert back to the "give me give me give me" model of love.

So naturally, in order to be able to give freely to others, we must first give to ourselves. But note the critical difference between *giving to oneself* and *seeking it from others*. It's kind of like an "ask not what others can do for you, but what you can do for yourself" philosophy. Also note that giving, at least in the sense I'm using the word, is not about providing oneself with material things or external achievements. Rather, it's about developing one's own emotional and intellectual resources. It's about investing in our own growth so that we may ultimately find within us the courage of self-acceptance and the desire to become more of who we are.

This is what psychotherapy aims to achieve. In my mind, therapy is not about changing people but rather about the opposite, that is, helping them to become more of who they are—specifically, by challenging them to uncover unknown parts of themselves. Naturally, psychotherapy doesn't have the exclusive rights for this kind of developmental journey. One can discover and articulate one's true voice in any human endeavor—just think of Cheryl Mendelson, the philosopher who wrote an 884-page book about housekeeping! A more obvious example, of course, is art—in whatever form. When you draw or write or take pictures you can't help but project your own vision, your own unique mind onto the picture.

In psychotherapy, the patient is the artist. Like Orpheus—the mythological poet whose mournful singing convinced Hades to send his dead wife back to the living—the patient descends into the underworld of lost love—his own unconscious—and using words, as well as nonverbal communications, he struggles to express his own unique pain, in his own unique idiom. Like any artist, the patient must employ both a creative impulse and a technique. The creative impulse, in the patient's case, consists of the wish to share something—to talk about a dream, a fight he had with his girlfriend, an argument with the boss, a sexual experience, or whatever. The technique involves his choice of what to share, in what words, at what time, and in what manner. In therapy, as in art, it's in the dialogue between these two things—impulse and technique, desire and discipline, emotion and cognition—that the articulation of personal vision can be found. In therapy, this is also where the solution to the problem of love can be found.

Throughout this book we will see that it's through this dialogue that my patients give themselves, or reclaim their own unique voice. And as we shall see, it's through this very attainment that they eventually liberate themselves from the patterns of failed love. Selfish as it may be, this attainment is what ultimately enables us to forsake the "give me give me give me" love paradigm and to replace its illusional consequences with the reality of giving ourselves to another person.

Now, while I will try to inspire you, the reader, to reach that level of love, I will also offer a practical road map—though by no means a quick-fix recipe—for getting there. As I explore the patterns of failed love, I will visit and revisit three basic steps you'll need to follow. These steps, which have grown out of my work with patients over the years, involve understanding your own psychology, so that you can clear your mind from tactical distractions and be more receptive to love. In Step One we recognize our relationships patterns and identify dating and relationship red flags so that we can stop our patterns in their tracks. In Step Two we learn about the ambivalence underlying our patterns—what it is we are personally ambivalent about. And in Step Three we resolve this ambivalence—by accepting it.

Taking into consideration the type of love pattern discussed and individual circumstances, these steps will repeat themselves with appropriate variations in each chapter of the book. At the same time, many of the examples and suggestions within each step can be used in any of the patterns discussed. In exploring these steps, I will illustrate not only how they unfold in the course of psychotherapy but also how to take them out of the consulting room and into your life.

As we shall soon see, these three steps are not merely a collection of technical tools but rather the practical application of the psychological prerequisites for attaining love. In mythology, the soul of the beloved is often represented by a butterfly because both go through a metamorphosis, which the ancient Greeks, in their infinite wisdom, considered to be a permanent attitude of the mind. In Step Three, rather than trying to catch or pin down another soul, we must engage our own. We must metamorphosize our own soul by giving to ourselves rather than expect others to give to us. Paradoxically when we do that we can also give to others, which is what love's all about.

As I walk you through the three steps I hope you'll find my patients' stories as emotionally compelling as I have and also easy to relate to so that you can indirectly learn from their successes and failures. While describing my work with patients, I will periodically slow down or freeze-frame the process, showing you how to apply my way of thinking and my therapeutic techniques to your own relationships and dating experiences.

Judging from my own work, as well that of colleagues and supervisees, I would estimate that at least 50 percent of the practice of any metropolitan area therapist consists of patients struggling with love. These include single individuals, who are striving to form an intimate relationship, as well as married or otherwise coupled patients, who are in crisis because love is not what they thought it would be. This "statistic," mind you, includes only those patients who are aware that their problem is love. If we add to it those who present with anxiety, depression, and psychosomatic illnesses—patients who often, though not always, develop symptoms as an unconscious attempt to solve the problem of love—I would venture to say that the vast majority of patients in psychotherapy are looking to cure their love ailments.

Needless to say, the search for love goes on well beyond the boundaries of the therapeutic arena, hence the vast number of self-help books about relationships. But while some of these books have been useful, even important, most failed to shed light on the problem of love. *Of course they failed*: the problem of love is as old as love itself! Indeed, where many quick-fix books failed was in promising too much too soon and in not helping the reader to work on his or her love problems *for the long-term*. They offered too many behavioral tactics and tips and not enough emotional strategic thinking.

But notwithstanding these false promises, these days more and more people in their late twenties and early thirties come into therapy already knowing that something is awry in their love life. These patients know that their relationship history involves a pattern that undermines their attempts to form a lasting commitment, and they know that they only have a few years to fix that problem. Also, in my experience fewer and fewer expect to be "cured" in three months. In my own generation of people in their forties, I find a change too. At least anecdotally, it seems that more than ever before, couples who are in a relationship crisis will seek marital counseling before resorting to separation and divorce. In my mind, this course of action reflects the realization that replacing one's partner does not solve the underlying problem of ambivalent love.

If the sixties and seventies promised liberation, spontaneity, and uninhibited fulfillment and the eighties countered with attractive though equally unrealistic remedies to those failed promises, the nineties have witnessed the reemergence of such concepts as duty, responsibility, and long-term planning, including the idea that love requires work. In the new millennium, I believe, we stand poised to finally integrate the discipline and orderliness that characterized love in the first half of the twentieth century, with the liberation and excitement brought to it by the second half. This is precisely the balanced approach to relationships I'm offering.

This book is based on my New York City practice, and as I discuss my cases we will encounter many examples of individuals struggling with age-old dynamics in a truly new world. We shall see that for many of them this means battling not only old, failed relationship patterns but also a new environment that paradoxically only serves to reinforce them. But this book is not antitechnology. Nor is it antispirituality. The information and the new age revolutions are merely part of its human landscape, adding a contemporary flavor to a new exploration of an old problem.

While Western civilization's notion that romantic love should lead to marriage and family is relatively new—replacing the concept of marriage as an economic or political institution only in the past one hundred to two hundred years—our quest for ambivalence-free, perfect romantic love is universal and ancient. By way of demonstrating that, and in order to help the reader grasp the essence of each of the relationship patterns discussed in the book, I have related each pattern to a classical story from Greek mythology.

When his wife, Eurydice, died, Orpheus, the Greek "father of the song," couldn't accept it. He was so stricken by the loss that he set out to search for Eurydice in Hades, the region of the dead. There, in the underworld, his mournful singing was so penetrating, so spellbinding, that he was allowed to retrieve his wife and bring her back to the land of the living. As a condition for her release, however, Orpheus had to promise that as Eurydice followed him through the underworld, he wouldn't look back at her until they came out on the other side. But of course, he *did* look—love made him look—and he therefore lost his wife again, this time for good. And it was all downhill from there, because as he refused to ever "date" anyone else, a group of women who felt neglected by him eventually attacked him. They tore his body apart and hurled his severed head in the river. Swept along by the river, the head called out, "Eurydice! Eurydice!" while the riverbanks echoed the name.

Among other things, this story is about the transformational powers of love—its powers to heal as well as to destroy. It would be nice to edit the story, for example, by cutting out the second half. Or by tacking on another ending, giving Orpheus yet another chance at love. Well, this is what I try to do with my psychotherapy patients and what I'd like to do for the reader of this book: give love yet another chance. Give it as many chances as necessary, since when it comes to love, the human mind is hardly a quick study. The good news, though, is that, at least conceptually, what we ought to do to get another chance is no mystery. But we get sidetracked by our compulsion to repeat what we already know and our fear of the truly spontaneous and new. In dating this happens when we become preoccupied with tactical concerns and veer off our strategic path. With such questions as "Should I call him or wait for him to call?" or "Should I give him more space or tell him what I feel when he pulls away?" we focus too much on the details of our interaction and lose sight of the bigger picture, which is that deep down we already know if this relationship is going somewhere. Deep down we *always* know when we are trapped in a failed relationship that we only keep alive with the inventive machinations of our denial.

Metamorphosizing love requires not only that we open our heart to the pain love has caused us but also that we open our eyes to the illusions it sold us. Getting in touch with our feelings is merely like a painter who accidentally drops a shape-less blob of color on the canvas and discovers he has just created art—it can't really happen without the intentionality of the act and the physical properties of the paint. Feelings, in other words, are not enough; we also need thoughts. We must feel, and we must think, and we must think about our feelings. In short, love must also think.

THE PATTERNS OF FAILED LOVE

To help you start the process of identifying your own patterns, I'd like to briefly review the most common relationship patterns, one at a time. For simplicity's sake, I have organized them into seven categories or types. Interestingly, these patterns exist in dating situations, sometimes even on a first date, as well as in long-term relationships, sometimes even in lifelong marriages. And as we shall see, these patterns only destine us to failure if we insist on not seeing them for what they are: fantasy, poetry, fairy tale, a passionate image of reality but not reality itself. To a cer-tain extent, each of these types resides comfortably as the cre-ative part of any love relationship. But then again, each is also fully capable of contaminating our psyche and of destroying our ability to form or sustain intimate relationships.

The first of the patterns I have called Narcissistic Love. It is only appropriate to start here, since, as conventional wisdom correctly assumes, loving oneself is a prerequisite to loving oth-ers, and in that sense all love begins with self-love. Indeed, we generally seek love because of how it makes *us* feel—alive, val-ued, and ecstatic about life, *our* life. So while a love relationship must involve a certain degree of healthy narcissism, in Narcissis-tic Love, our need to feel special is out of whack. Whereas falling in love requires that we idealize our partner so that we are not too bothered by his limitations, in Narcissistic Love, the gap between this idealization and the reality of the other person is so wide that it is ultimately unsustainable.

The couple in this love pattern seems to thrive on the notion that their relationship is the ultimate, most extraordinary expression of love. This is the couple who looks and acts like each other's greatest love at each and every moment. When we are in this kind of a relationship we imbue everything we do or have, and especially our partner, with such aesthetic, intellectual, or emotional exclusivity that it makes everyone else feel inadequate. In a long-term relationship, this type of mutual idealization often reveals itself to be a superficial posture hiding a Pandora's box of secret resentments, sexual problems, or extramarital affairs. In a dating situation, this degree of idealization is temporary, and it frequently leads to its opposite, devaluation. One of the questions I will discuss in relation to this pattern is how to distinguish the healthy and necessary idealization that characterizes the initial "honeymoon" period of a relationship (and which hopefully is also present later on) from the more problematic idealization described above. As a preview, let me just say that while the former merely makes us feel better about ourselves, the latter is an all-out, if unconscious, attempt to regulate our self-esteem.

In the second relationship pattern, Virtual Love, we engage in a relationship with a built-in geographical separation such as a long-distance, intermittent, or online relationship. We are thus physically prevented from being together with the other person on a regular basis. Unencumbered by the reality of everyday life, in its extreme form, this kind of romantic arrangement fosters a fantasy of perfection about the other person and the relationship. But as soon as we try to bring this "virtual" love into the physical world, our fantastical construction is shattered, leaving us with pangs of longing and a disturbing sense of mistrust in our capacity for love.

In the third pattern, One-Way Love, the more unavailable the other person is, the more we long for him or her. When we are in love with someone who won't respond, we tell ourselves that if he or she only returned our love, we'd be happy and fulfilled. But the truth is that when this kind of love does get reciprocated, we often lose interest. Furthermore, as we shall see, the flip side of pursuing unavailable people—that is, being ourselves unavailable to those who pursue us—is part and parcel of the same pattern.

In Forbidden Love, we are actually drawn to the sense of risk and even danger created by the obstacles standing in the way of the relationship. A high school teacher and his student fall madly in love with each other. A divorced woman falls in love with her son's college buddy. A married woman falls in love with her tennis instructor or her therapist. Now, while in these situations we believe that if we could only survive or remove the forbidding obstacle, we'd be able to actualize our love for good, in most cases, it's this very forbidden element that fuels the passion. So when it is removed, the love usually dies from within as one or both lovers get bored or distracted by other forbidden circumstances.

The fifth pattern of failed love, Sexual Love, defined not as love with a sexual component but rather a sexual component without love, is a relationship based on sexual desire and not much else. This can come in a conscious form, as when the two parties engage in physical exploration with no strings attached, or unconsciously, where one or both parties delude themselves that they are in love, which is all too common in the case of men who are often really "in lust." In either situation, the relationship falls apart when one or both partners "remember" that they are not only bodies and that their psyche or soul has as much reality and just as powerful needs as do their sexual and sensual organs.

In Triangular Love, we bring another person, real or imaginary, into our relationship. For example, we love our spouse as a wife/mother but love our mistress as a sexual partner. Or we date someone while secretly having a crush on his brother. Or we love our husband but prefer to spend every weekend with our mother. This third party, incidentally, is not always a person—it can be a thing or an activity. We may be committed to our girlfriend but spend all our weekends skiing with the guys or drinking. Or maybe we love our girlfriend but prefer to spend all our free time on eBay or e-trade or some other online outfit. In most of these cases, when push comes to shove, it's that third party that ends up being cast away but not before damaging the primary relationship. Sometimes both the primary and the "extracurricular" relationships fail, and in some cases the primary relationship even loses out to the competition. But then, as in Forbidden Love, we are likely to find out that the competitor's intense appeal was all but an illusion.

Finally, in Androgynous Love, we unconsciously want our partner to have an emotional sex-change operation. "Men are dicks" or "Women are too sensitive," we say, as we try to change our partner, wishing he were more like a woman or she were more like a man—a clear recipe for disaster. Or we might in fact choose someone who is more like our own gender. In these post-feminist times, many of us end up in a dating pattern or a relationship where the woman is an aggressive go-getter and the man a sensitive, emotional type. When these roles are truly polarized, the relationship is in trouble because sooner or later the man will start resenting the woman for being an unfeeling drill sergeant, and the woman will look down on the man for being a passive doormat.

While we all know someone—if not ourselves—who is

gripped by the repetitive nature of one of these patterns, it's important to remember that when they aren't extreme, these patterns are simply various aspects of love. And not only do they all exist in some way in all relationships, but as I mentioned earlier, even when they are destructive, they rarely come in a pure form. Take the case of Betsy, a woman in her early thirties who came to see me after a series of unsuccessful relationships. Betsy's first serious boyfriend during college was a slightly older medical intern. Energetic, idealistic, dedicated, and sensitive, this man meant the world to her. He had a whole philosophy of relating to his patients, would volunteer his time to work in underdeveloped countries, and was always engaged in "important" research projects. For the first couple of years she was able to feel special merely by being with him and supporting him, and he experienced her as someone who made him feel loved and cared for. But with time, he began to perceive her as needy—someone who would take him away from his research and for whom he would have to forsake more challenging, glamorous women. This, of course, made Betsy feel bad about herself, but she loved him and couldn't imagine life without him. Eventually, he broke up with her and she subsequently vowed never again to fall for this type of Narcissistic Love. Of course, this was not her term for it, and it was also only years later while in therapy that she realized she actually had two similar, though much shorter, relationships earlier in life.

But at the time, having been hurt so much from the breakup, Betsy decided to take a break from serious relationships. In her midtwenties now, she dated here and there and at some point developed a strong sexual attraction for Bob, a handsome, young-looking law student she met in a bar. He was equally attracted to her and they quickly developed an intense sexual relationship but with the clear and open understanding that this was just for fun and that neither of them was looking for a commitment. While they were always pleasant and sweet to each other, they would only get together once or twice a week in the evening to fool around. At Bob's initiative, they would role-play different sexual fantasies such as nurse and doctor or a scenario in which she would beg him to have sex with her and he would finally relent. Though Betsy enjoyed and in fact craved these experiences, eventually she began to feel he was using her, and once again she started to feel bad about herself.

At about that time, Eric, a friend of her roommate, was visiting from California. Betsy spent one night talking to him about relationships and her situation with Bob. This man was so much deeper and more complex than Bob that she found herself being drawn to him on every level. She then stopped seeing Bob and started e-mailing and talking on the phone with Eric. When she subsequently went to see him for a long weekend in Los Angeles, they had wonderful conversations and became romantically involved. This quickly developed into a full-fledged, long-distance relationship lasting close to a year before the issue of commitment came up. Eric was in the entertainment industry and said it was unrealistic for him to leave LA. Betsy, on the other hand, had just started her first New York job after graduate school and was therefore prepared to consider moving to LA if he would commit to the relationship. But as soon as he heard she was willing to move "for him," Eric began to feel burdened by the responsibility. "I'm not ready to commit," he said, and that ushered in an additional long-distance year, one full of repeated discussions, doubts, hurt feelings, disappointments, and anger. "You are a wonderful person," Eric finally told Betsy, "and I guess I want to want to commit to you, but I just can't." They broke up and Betsy was once again devastated.

So here we see someone who was grappling with three of the patterns. In trying to overcome Narcissistic Love, she fell into the temporarily intoxicating pleasures of Sexual Love; and in trying to find more meaningful intimacy she was lured by the promise of Virtual Love. In each relationship, Betsy thought she was trying something new, and in a sense, she was—each of these relationships had its own distinct features. But as is intuitively evident to any observer, the new was just another version of the old. Indeed, Betsy kept falling into a paradoxical trap: the apparent differences between these relationships were precisely what enabled her to repeatedly choose the similarity of failure. But it wasn't only that her disappointments were similar. Rather, on closer examination, the three relationship patterns are causally related. They all spring out of one critical and universal problem, that of ambivalence.

If we examine the patterns of failed love I've described, we can see that a similar mechanism—an attempt to avoid feelings of vulnerability and therefore hate, anger, or resentment toward the object of our love—operates in each and every one. In Narcissistic Love, ambivalence is temporarily or superficially escaped by means of mutual idealization, whose purpose is to avoid facing the imperfections of the other person and how they make you feel. In Virtual Love, the negative side of the ambivalence—the hate or other negative feelings—yields to the age-old paradoxical principle that absence makes the heart grow fonder. In this kind of relationship, our love for the other person remains pure because, in one way or another, he or she is physically absent. In One-Way Love, I say hello, you say good-bye—so I avoid ambivalence by means of longing for what I can't have. And of course, if by some chance I get it, I lose interest, which is to say, I still avoid ambivalence—now I only have negative feelings. In Forbidden Love, the negative emotions are projected onto external factors or people who are the enemies of our love and who prevent us from fully realizing it.

In Sexual Love, we split our ambivalence so that we are compelled by the body, but not by the soul, of our partner. In Trian-

gular Love, we split our ambivalence between our primary partner and another person or activity we bring into the relationship.
Rather than living with our partner's shortcomings, we find a
third party who doesn't have them or, more accurately, who has
different shortcomings. Or instead of dealing with the boredom
in our marriage, we compulsively pursue such external activities
as drinking, shopping, and golfing. And in Androgynous Love,
we try to avoid ambivalence by pretending that there are no psychological differences between the sexes and that our partner
can therefore be completely compatible with us; when he is not,
we pretend he can be changed. Or we try to escape our ambivalence about men (or women) by picking someone who is more
feminine (masculine).

It is perhaps easy to understand why we would be willing to
delude ourselves in so many ways in order to avoid feeling
ambivalent—who in their right mind would want to feel anger,
disapproval, contempt, or disgust toward their partner? What is
not so obvious, though, is whether or not we are doomed to
struggle with ambivalence in all our love relationships. And to
the extent that we do, is there a better alternative to self-deluded
love? What is it? To answer these questions, we have to delve
even further into the patterns of failed love and to apply in each
case my three-step approach to attaining love.

1

Narcissistic Love

There was nothing Echo would ever say more gladly,
"Let us get together!"
OVID

We are all familiar with the story of Narcissus, the beautiful youth who fell in love with his own reflection in the pool. But we are less familiar with the story of his partner, Echo, the young nymph who was cursed by the gods to only be able to repeat, never initiate, speech. At one point, when Echo—whose heart was never deterred by her beloved's self-absorption—came upon Narcissus and heard him uttering words of love, she naturally repeated his words. To the outside observer this would surely look like a mutual love fest. The truth, of course, was that Narcissus was talking to his own reflection in the pool and that Echo was merely being an audio version of that reflective pool. But even more interesting, Narcissus and Echo were *themselves* fooled by this house of mirrors: since from where she stood she couldn't see the reflection in the pool, Echo thought Narcissus was talking to her, while Narcissus—his gaze transfixed by his own image in the pool—took Echo's voice to be that of his beloved reflection, whose lips clearly moved to the same words of love.

It's probably no coincidence that Narcissus is far better known than Echo. After all, seeking the limelight is what he's all about. When you think about it, though, the character of Echo is no stranger to us either. The feminists see her in the supportive role of the traditional wife, the woman behind the man. And pop psychologists describe her as the codependent or the enabler—the selfless spouse who takes care, and unwittingly participates in the undoing, of her selfishly self-destructive partner (Narcissus ended up dying of starvation because he wouldn't leave his reflection). But what's less known about Echo and her contemporary versions is that even though she appears to be Narcissus's opposite, she is actually every bit as narcissistic as he is. Traditionally, women in our culture were socialized to support and respect, if not obey, their men. They were supposed to attain high self-esteem not through an external achievement of their own but rather through the nurturing of others. In terms of child rearing, there may well be a biological predisposition for this in women—more so than in men. The point is that even as our society evolves, many women still make themselves feel good about themselves by making others feel good about themselves. In other words, their selfish need is to be selfless. Their narcissism lies in the fact that they need to be needed—regardless of whether or not the other person actually needs them. So their narcissism, while harder to detect, is just as pronounced as a man's might be.

In Narcissistic Love, the couple's dynamic often follows these gender-based forms of narcissism. The man is out there building Trump Towers, and the woman applauds and supports the effort by taking care of the home and by looking good in his arms. In a dating context, notwithstanding all the changes brought about by the women's movement, the same assumption might be operating within the couple; that is, the man is the gifted, brilliant, important player—the lawyer, banker, architect, actor, doctor, or artist—whose work, mission, or schedule takes precedence over the woman's, regardless of her work, career, or other overtly selfish desires. As upsetting as this might be to contemplate in this day and age, many women with significant achievements do not feel good about themselves—that is, they suffer from low self-esteem—if they are not needed by a partner or a child and if they are not socially pleasing to others.

These gender dynamics are not as rigid or fixed as you might expect, and as we shall see, they can flip. In addition, many people—men and women—follow a love path that takes them from a relationship in which they are the Echo to one in which they are the Narcissus, before finally ending up somewhere in the middle.

STEP ONE: RECOGNIZING YOUR PATTERN

While we usually think of "pathological" narcissism as a form of excessive self-love, the truth is almost the opposite. Driven by unconscious low self-esteem or self-hate, the narcissist strives to feel good about himself by exaggerating and showing off his achievement, power, or beauty. In addition, the more consciously self-hating or low-self-esteem individual is just as much of a narcissist, for he too is self-involved in his relentless quest to feel good about himself. It is thus more accurate to think of narcissism as the self-centeredness resulting from our efforts to *regulate our self-esteem*. It is also important to appreciate that narcissism is not only a pathological condition but also a necessary and potentially positive aspect of psychological development. In motivating us to be productive or to please others, the drive to attain high self-esteem actually facilitates growth. Of course, when extreme, and under certain conditions, it does become a debilitating problem.

Similarly, narcissism plays an important positive and negative role in the phenomenon of falling in love. Since our self-esteem evolves from early childhood and onward out of the experience of being loved, when we fall in love it is immediately engaged. If our love is reciprocated we feel valued; if not, we feel inadequate. And because maintaining a high self-esteem is so crucial to our sense of well-being, our narcissism employs various defense mechanisms to that end. Chief among these and most relevant to the experience of falling in love is the defense of *idealization.* The emotional generosity we feel when we fall in love is made possible by the way we idealize our partner. This idealization enables us to ignore his imperfections, to believe we have finally met our soul mate, and to trust that he will not betray or abandon us. We often don't really know this person when we fall in love and we have no factual basis to justify this attitude. But it nonetheless makes us feel valued, vital, and special—amid a vast sea of humanity in relation to which we are quite ordinary, unseen, and inconsequential. In short, idealization makes us feel good about ourselves, directly when we are idealized, or indirectly when we idealize someone else and bask in his reflection.

In lasting, more or less "healthy" relationships, this type of idealization is present sometimes—often dominating the early phases of a relationship, the "honeymoon" period, when we are also in love with love. But with time it is informed by the process of getting to know the other person. Diluted in some ways, enriched in others, it is influenced by the reality of the partner's mind and body and by the accumulated history of our togetherness. While a kernel of the early idealization must remain if love's to last, the intensity and expansiveness of the initial falling in love are ultimately inconsistent with lasting intimacy. This is so because if we cannot show our less attractive qualities and have them registered as such by the other person, we aren't quite known to him and therefore are loved only superficially, which is what Narcissistic Love is all about. In the best-case scenario of Narcissistic Love we fall in love with *something* in the person, fixate our gaze on it and insist that's the *whole* person. As a result, we don't really get to know our partner up front, which often means we later find out he has some kind of a secret or unspoken life.

One of my patients, an attractive, articulate woman in her late twenties, nonetheless came across as somewhat fragmented or lacking in focus and self-confidence. In childhood, she was very close to her mother, but her father was absent, literally because at some point her parents divorced but also emotionally because he was, as she put it, "a nonentity." On top of being quiet and withdrawn, he was also somewhat infantile and naive, often making stupid jokes or mumbling irrelevant things. Finally, he was also a "failure," as he was unemployed during much of the patient's childhood. None of this bothered the patient, she would always say. "Since I never had a relationship with him in the first place, I don't have feelings about him one way or another." But of course, as I would always tell her, her lack of relationship with her father was the most critical aspect of her relationship with her father. In other words, it's not really possible to not have a relationship with one's parent—at least in fantasy. At the very least, the parent's absence is always a huge presence in the person's mind and in his or her intimate relationships. For this patient, the absence made itself present in a series of relationships with idealized, narcissistic men.

Like many in her place, this woman would consciously and consistently choose men who were *anything but* her father: professional, smart, passionate, sensitive, and good listeners—in short, men who appeared to be perfect and whom, unlike her father, she could easily idealize. The problem is, not only is no one perfect, but also those who appear to be are usually even less perfect than the rest of us. For example, one of her relationships was with a young lawyer who worked as a legal-aid attorney in a public agency. He was assertive and smart, as you might expect from someone in his field, but also idealistic about his work, which involved advocating for poor inner-city folk. He was also very attractive in a boyish sort of way. He was affectionate and considerate and he enjoyed talking about family and relationship issues. Finally, he was fun-loving and always up for traveling and socializing.

The relationship started with intimate talks into the night, long daily phone conversations, open and frequent sexual exploration, and mutual proclamations that this was different from any other relationships they'd had. After a month they practically moved in together, though Kevin would occasionally go back to his place. Yet a couple of months later, Kevin started talking about needing some time to wind down on his own from his stressful, demanding job, as well as "needing some space." This seemed reasonable enough to my patient, so they agreed they would spend less time together during week nights. Correspondingly, however, sex became less frequent and a few times Kevin couldn't get an erection. But even then he continued to talk about their relationship, his anxieties, and his wish for the relationship to work out. "It really has nothing to do with you," he said. "It's *my* issue." And he went further, saying his need for space was probably a reaction to having been raised by a smothering, overprotective mother. And he was interested in my patient's feelings, wanting to make sure she didn't personalize it.

Even though Kevin was pulling back, my patient continued to feel he was very special indeed. He took responsibility for his problems, validated her feelings, and, unlike most men, was truly communicative. So while she was constantly feeling his absence—even when he was there she was beginning to worry that he wanted to get away—she "decided" not to be needy but rather to help him gets *his* needs met. When they made plans she would sensitively ask if he was sure he didn't want to do his own thing, and she would sometimes bring him dinner and then leave or would spend time with him on the weekends accompanying him while he ran his errands. In addition, when they spent nights together she would always accommodate his sexual requests. It wasn't only that she wanted to make it easier for him to be with her; it was also that she truly enjoyed every minute she spent with him. "He is so knowledgeable and insightful," she told me. "And he opened so many intellectual and emotional doors for me that it's hard for me to imagine not being with him."

But my patient's efforts to be positive and to deny her negative feelings, coupled with her idealization of Kevin, backfired when after about a year and a half he suddenly broke up with her, sensitively explaining that he had been feeling too ambivalent all along and that he finally realized it wouldn't be fair to her to continue the relationship if he couldn't commit. My patient was stunned. What about "wanting to work it out" and "it's my issues" and "you are so special," she said, demanding an explanation. "Why do you want me to get into it? I don't want to hurt your feelings!" he responded. But when she continued to press him, he mumbled and blushed and hesitantly started to explain that after the first few weeks he "lost" his sexual feelings for her and that he had to fantasize about other women to be able to perform, and that, yes, it *was* his problem, because it had happened to him before and that he was trying to work it out and see if his feelings would return, but they didn't. "I'm sorry," he said, hiding his contorting face in his hands in what appeared to my patient to be—for the very first and the last time—a pathetic expression of shame and inadequacy.

It took my patient several months to get over the rejection and loss but even longer to begin to see who Kevin really was. When she did, she saw that in addition to—or should we say underneath—his probably truly special personality, there was also an insecure, dependent, conflicted child who could "talk the talk" but not "walk the walk." She also then realized that his ideals, for example, working in legal aid where he made little money representing the underdog—while admirable in and of themselves—were motivated not by true passion but by his fear of growing up and dealing with the "real world."

Whoever the "real" Kevin was—and maybe there is no such thing as the real person in the first place—when she was in love, my patient could only see a part of the picture, the part allowing her to be involved with someone so special that she herself could feel special merely by association. This is typical of Narcissistic Love: we deny our ambivalence about the other person in order to escape our own low self-esteem. In this case, my patient's low self-esteem was clearly a result of how her father made her feel—not worthy of his presence. But since she was not conscious of the impact of his inadequacy and absence on her—only of her wish to avoid the impact by staying away from any man appearing inadequate in the slightest—she ended up with men who looked perfect but, paradoxically though inescapably, were in fact desperate enough to go to great lengths to cover up deep feelings of inadequacies. With time, each of these men's beautiful packaging would chip and crack, sooner or later showing they were too good to be true, and ironically, each time she would end up being rejected by or rejecting these men who would ultimately behave very much like her father.

After the breakup with Kevin, the patient worked in therapy on understanding these dynamics. But while she began to comprehend it intellectually, it took her one more relationship to get it emotionally. Although my three-step approach involves the application of thoughts to feelings, this application cannot be forced, and each step must ultimately be known emotionally, not just cognitively. For this patient, the emotional awareness of Step One, Recognizing Your Pattern, came after another, yearlong relationship, in which, by way of trying not to repeat her mistake with Kevin, she chose someone who was clearly honest and sincere, with absolutely no likelihood of a hidden agenda. The problem was that she now glorified this man's sincerity, thinking of it as an extremely rare and rarefied characteristic. In short, in idealizing a quality that is perhaps a necessary, but certainly not a sufficient, condition for a good relationship, she once again sought to be part of something extraordinary. So predictably enough, when this initial idealization waned, she found herself bored in the relationship. It was only when she broke up with him that she realized she had actually repeated the narcissistic aspect of her relationship with Kevin.

It was at that point, when I told her that both relationships were based on her understandable, if self-defeating, need to escape feelings of low self-esteem stemming from her relationship with her father, that she got Step One emotionally. "I have to look in the mirror," she said, "and accept the fact that I'm not the most beautiful woman in New York, that I'm feeling bad about myself, and that no man can ever make me feel what my father didn't—that I'm the most special thing in the world." She vowed to never again date a man in order to feel special.

IDEALIZATION AND DEVALUATION

In some relationships or dating situations, our tendency to idealize the other person is met with reality's fierce resistance early on, and in these cases our idealization typically turns into its opposite, devaluation. One of my patients, a smart, introspective young architect, met his girlfriend, Joan, at a party. "She was not exactly my type," he explained. "She was short and not as pretty or sexy as I would normally go for, you know, she had glasses, plus, she was older, like thirty-eight. But I was drawn to her when I heard her talking to someone about the *Four Last Songs* of Strauss. Do you know that music? It's the most beautiful, truly spiritual music ever composed—Strauss wrote it before he died and it's all about life and death. It's one of my favorites, so I immediately felt a connection with her. So I joined the conversation and we talked about it, and then the other people left, and, get this, the first thing she tells me is she's going to Tibet! Can you believe this? You know that I was thinking of going to Tibet and have studied Tibetan art. And then we talked about philosophy—she turned out to be a philosophy professor—and it turns out her whole thing is Spinoza, who was my favorite philosopher in college! So obviously, there was an incredible connection there and we spent the rest of the night talking, and then we spent almost every night together for the next two weeks. And she really got what I'm trying to achieve professionally and how I want to integrate spirituality and design."

This patient grew up as an only child in an upper-middle-class family that was extremely disciplined, structured, and conventional. Both his parents were corporate types who were devoted to doing the right thing, working hard and providing the family a stable, financially secure future. Almost like Captain Von Trapp from *The Sound of Music,* his parents had no patience for silliness, creativity, curiosity, or playfulness. Even fun things had to be done in the "right way" and artistic endeavors such as piano lessons were never about subjective expression but rather about order and repetition. And all messes—if there ever were any—had to be cleaned immediately. Therefore, as a child—and remember, all children, if anything, are silly artists—the patient felt unseen, unvalued, and oppressed. So as a teenager, and later as an adult, he felt compelled to seek self-expression outside of the family, literally and figuratively, in writing, listening to music, spirituality, and generally all those subjective things that were so foreign to his parents and forbidden in his childhood.

When he met Joan, he felt validated. Here was someone older

and smarter who dedicated her life to questioning conventions and seeking spiritual meaning and who loved exactly the same stuff he did. And for their first two weeks together, the couple elaborated on these similarities, listening to Strauss in solemn silence, discussing the meaning of deity in Spinoza and transcending reality itself in euphoric sexual unions. But then Joan abruptly lost her job. Although when he first heard about it, my patient was completely supportive and upset on Joan's behalf, when they continued to talk about it over the next few days, he began to see that this didn't come out of nowhere. Joan had been turned down for a tenure-track position and apparently had a record of not finishing academic papers and not showing up to seminars she was teaching.

"I guess she is not quite on top of things," he first thought. "I wonder how this will affect our relationship." And then: "Philosophy and music are one thing, but you have to make a living, you have to be responsible, and you have to have your priorities right." Not wanting to upset Joan, he did not mention these thoughts to her, and in addition, Joan was much more interested in continuing their philosophical conversations than talking about her job situation. This, of course, further alarmed my patient, as he began to feel that his new girlfriend was simply out of touch with reality. "She has a great mind," he said, "but I have to say—and I don't know why I didn't see it before—I think she is a flake. Also—and I don't know why I didn't see *that* before—she's kind of unattractive." And he broke up the relationship.

Well, the reason he didn't see these things before was that the line between idealization and devaluation is even thinner than the one between love and hate. Both idealization and devaluation are based on denying aspects of a person's character, a denial that stems from our struggle to regulate our self-esteem. In the case of this patient, the idealization "kicked in" when Joan totally validated the part of his personality that was neither seen nor valued in his childhood by his parents. With Joan, he was the silly, dreamy, creative child—but a celebrated one, more of a genius than a kid—whom his parents completely rejected. But when this came into conflict with reality, the patient "flipped" into his parents' perspective, according to which, play, spirituality, and subjectivity are flaky and pathetic. This did not surprise me because, even though the patient's spiritual or artistic interests were genuine, unconsciously in his mind they were always associated with low self-esteem. While consciously he had rebelled against his parents' conventional rigidity and chose a more creative path, deeper in his mind, his parents remained the ultimate yardstick and judge of acceptability. According to this yardstick—which, notwithstanding his resistance to it, he had naturally internalized as a child—tough-minded practicality, discipline, success and money, not philosophy, are what counted. And this viewpoint entered the picture when reality deperfected Joan, rendering her no longer capable of making him feel good about himself.

So in this brief relationship, the patient switched from experiencing himself as an idealized child to a powerful parent. And correspondingly, Joan had turned in his mind from being a powerful, validating parent to a weak, impractical child. In other words, the patient never experienced Joan the person, beyond the psychic function she fulfilled for him as projected, symbolic aspects of himself. This is typical of Narcissistic Love, where our partner's main emotional purpose is to play a role in our internal world, regardless of who he really is. This role—you should know this by now—is to help us to boost our self-esteem. It was thus no coincidence that my patient ended up feeling good about himself both in idealizing and in devaluing his girlfriend, first by associating himself with an idealized person and then by dissociating himself from a devalued person. Another way to put it is that as long as Joan was the "good mirror," in which he saw what he loved about himself, he was madly in love, but when she then turned into the "bad mirror," reflecting what he hated in himself, he fell out of love.

BATTLING NARCISSUS AND ECHO

Because falling in love always involves some idealization, and because the subjective experience of being in love is not fundamentally different in Narcissistic Love than in more "realistic" falling in love—Freud once described the state of falling in love as akin to a brief psychotic episode, and Shakespeare wrote about lunatics, lovers, and madmen—it is particularly difficult to identify the markers of Narcissistic Love early on, in real time. It can therefore be a real struggle to reach Step One and catch yourself idealizing someone and/or being idealized, not in order to have a relationship with another imperfect human being, but rather as a means of feeling good about yourself. Nonetheless, in addition to the sheer repetition of the pattern—which ultimately is the best, if retroactive, indication that your infatuations and idealizations do not stand the tests of time and reality—there are a few clues that can help.

Sometimes clichés are really true, and the one about a man's midlife crisis and the accompanying desire for a younger woman could well be such a case. In my practice I've seen men in their forties or fifties who are unable to come to terms with their limitations—this is often the age in life when you reach some sort of a glass ceiling, in your career, health, or sexuality—and therefore fall in love with a young woman who represents youth, vitality, hope, and perhaps immortality. Not only is she more attractive, but being young she also tends to idealize the man, which at least momentarily helps him transcend his limitations and feel better about himself.

Perhaps the flip side of this cliché is that of the younger woman who falls in love with a powerful or wealthy man and convinces herself that she is attracted to his "strong personality." In this case the woman often enjoys the jewelry, gifts, and royal treatment not because they are a sign of his love but rather a sign that she has value. Looking good or having a lavish lifestyle makes her feel not loved, but worthy. In all likelihood, this woman grew up feeling insignificant or only conditionally loved. So the general principle here is that if your partner somehow saves you from yourself, that is, if there is something about him that helps you to escape bad feelings about yourself, this might well be Narcissistic Love.

But isn't this the whole point of love, I hear you saying, that it makes us feel valued and therefore full of life and happy? Well, there are two answers to this question. First, it's a matter of degree. In other words, as I've said about all patterns of failed love, the difference between Narcissistic Love and plain old falling in love is in some sense quantitative, not qualitative. So the greater the discrepancy between our previous sense of self and our current, while in love, the greater the chances that we are using the other person for our internal narcissistic reasons. The second answer is that in more realistic love what makes us feel valued is the connection with the other person, not the external goods they bring to our life. In Narcissistic Love, on the other hand, we can't quite be certain that if our partner suddenly lost his money or power or health or youth, we would still want to be with him.

In terms of dating, if you and/or the person you are seeing are generally more concerned with *images* or *ideas* of reality then with reality itself, chances are you are more susceptible to Narcissistic Love. For example, someone who has a fixed aesthetic standard that people or even objects must conform to is more likely to fall in love with appearance than with substance. This is not to say that appearance is not important in our society or that it doesn't play a major role in sexual attractiveness—it sure is, and there's no point trying to deny it. It's just that it's not the essential ingredient for falling or staying in love. Likewise, someone who loves working for a powerful boss because it's prestigious, not because she likes working with this particular person, or someone who goes to the opera because it's considered sophisticated rather than because she enjoys the music—is more likely to fall in love with an idea of who the other person is, as opposed to the reality. Again, this is not to say that any of us is beyond the idea of impressing others. Who among us would not feel good about knowing a celebrity, being on TV, or having a "cool" job? On balance, though, we hopefully end up doing more of what *we* like or value than what others would consider impressive. If we generally don't, or if we date someone who doesn't, we are more susceptible to Narcissistic Love.

A related indication of Narcissistic Love is when our feelings for our date or partner change in accordance with how he is viewed by others. So if your parents or a friend you respect really like your new boyfriend, and in response to that you feel a surge of love for him, chances are you are more concerned with your image than with your boyfriend's substance. This is probably true even if your feelings change in the opposite direction, that is, if you find yourself liking your boyfriend less in response to positive feedback from others. In this case you are still responding to what others think—in rebellion or in some other contrary fashion—and not out of your own impulse toward your partner.

While the Narcissus among us may recognize his concern with image or ideas as described above, if you tend to be more of the Echo, you may appropriately and ironically recognize only your partner above. So how to see your own susceptibility to Narcissistic Love? Well, representing perhaps a traditional male point of view, Rilke, the poet, wrote, "I hold this to be the highest task of a bond between two people: that each should stand guard over the solitude of the other." This is surely where Echo fails, because for her, solitude means being alone with her low self-esteem and she is therefore only happy when in the company of her idealized lover. So if you are generally someone who can't tolerate being alone—which means your own mind or life is of little interest to you—you might well be predisposed to Narcissistic Love. More specifically, if you feel you can't stay away from the person you are dating—physically or even emotionally in the sense that you can't stop thinking about him— chances are you're in the throes of Narcissistic Love.

Consistent with the above, if you are generally a giving, supportive person who avoids center stage and thrives on taking care of others, you are naturally at risk for Narcissistic Love. The more you are this way with your partner and the more he enjoys the limelight, the greater the risk. Although narcissistic men come in various forms, there are two common types that you may want to watch for: the man who is single-mindedly, and to the exclusion of everything else, preoccupied with his career or with the accumulation of wealth and male toys, and the man who exudes a seductive, childlike charm, excessive idealism or sensuality, and a profound desire to be loved even by people he doesn't know.

Narcissistic women too come in a variety of their own. Notwithstanding the changes in our society of the past thirty years, traditional forms of female narcissism still abound. In addition to the common Echo type discussed above, women, more so than men, continue to attempt to improve their self-esteem by improving their appearance. So men who wish to avoid Narcissistic Love should watch for women with extreme aesthetic preoccupations, women who always dress like models or who decorate their homes like a museum. Men and women should also wonder about potential partners who have "special" or un-usual gifts and talents, not actual talents (such as artistic, mathe-matical, or mechanical aptitudes) but rather some kind of select, transcendental spirituality or claims of supernatural abilities. And of course, since we have traveled some distance in the past century, let's not forget that "male" and "female" narcissism are no longer in the exclusive domain of each gender. Also, these "types" are only intended as clues, to be examined in the context of your own, hopefully increased, self-awareness. None of them in and of themselves represents a narcissistic personality, and cer-tainly not "pathological" narcissism. Obviously, there is nothing inherently wrong or alarming in having a passion for one's career or for aesthetics or for taking care of others or for spirituality.

Another possible sign of Narcissistic Love is when your rela-tionship is isolated from the rest of your life or your partner's. He takes you to wonderful places—restaurants, shows, vacations—but doesn't want to meet your friends or for you to meet his fam-ily. Or he might want to meet your friends, but they can't relate to him and so you end up distancing yourself from or losing your close friends. Or if because of your new love you act like—and assuming you are not one—a teenager, meaning you neglect other responsibilities and only do "wild" things with your lover. I would also be suspicious of overnight transformations owing to love—for example, if under the idealized influence of a new boyfriend or girlfriend you suddenly develop a passion for art, music, the law, physics, writing, wine, marijuana, or really any-thing that wasn't quite you yesterday. Of course, this is not to say that we should not learn from or be influenced by our partner. It's the sudden, chameleon-like (though often genuinely experi-enced) transformation that I'm talking about.

Finally, as we saw earlier, one of the reasons it's difficult to identify Narcissistic Love in real time is because even when we repeat the pattern, we may idealize a different aspect of the partner in each different relationship. In fact, paradoxically enough, we sometimes do that on purpose to avoid repeating the pattern. So after dating and getting hurt by an investment banker whom we idealized for his vigor, assertiveness, and ambition, we turn to date a social worker whom we now idealize for his sensitivity, honesty, and availability. In both cases, if we idealize too much, we are bound to end up with the experience of "he's not the person I thought he was." But therein lies this clue to Narcissistic Love: if we are first compelled and then repelled by one thing and its opposite, perhaps the problem is not in those things but rather in how we perceive them. To generalize, realizing that the problem is our perception of reality, not reality itself, is the essence of reaching Step One. Rather than treating the other person as a mirror, first good, then bad, we turn to a symbolic mirror inside our mind and say to ourselves, "Mirror, mirror on the wall, *I'm not* the prettiest of them all."

STEP TWO: UNDERSTANDING YOUR AMBIVALENCE

There's a poignant moment in the original Greek myth, when Narcissus repeatedly reaches to embrace or kiss the object of his pining, only to discover, with great anxiety, that as his beloved attempts to reciprocate, he suddenly disappears in the water. In the context of real-life Narcissistic Love, this anxiety is not only about the inevitable loss of love but also about the loss of a mirror upon which we depend for the regulation of our self-esteem. When the relationship is over—or in the case of a long-term relationship, when the intense idealization is over—we not only feel bad about ourselves but also confused, not knowing what we want from a relationship. While extremely painful, this is not a bad moment. On the contrary, seized correctly, it can be the beginning of Step Two, in which we ask ourselves what it is, other than an external regulator of our self-esteem, that we want from an intimate relationship with another person. We now know that we can't have perfection—only a false mirror can offer that—so to fine tune the question, we must ask, What kind of human imperfection can we live with? Naturally, to answer this question we need to know more about ourselves—we need a more or less objective psychological mirror.

Short of psychotherapy—which is not always necessary and in any event is not for everyone—we can only find this knowledge by being involved in life, seeking experiences and relationships and then reflecting on them. One patient did this by comparing his experience of two different types of relationships. The patient, Joel, was a young computer programmer with a strong intellectual bent. In one type of relationship, he would get involved with women who seemed sincere, kind, and easygoing, all qualities that he felt were critical for a long-term relationship. But in each case, a couple of months into the relationship, these qualities would turn into "naive," "simple," and "unsophisticated," which was a problem because the patient truly enjoyed an intellectual conversation and had keen interests in literature, history, and politics. Therefore, each time he would break up with what he eventually came to call "the flower girls," he would look for the opposite type and would get involved with what—he informed me—a *New York Times* Style section article called a "psycho chick." These were sophisticated, sexy, captivating women, who, you may have guessed, a couple of months into the relationship would become "difficult," "hostile," and "unstable." So they would end up being equally unworkable.

Naturally, it took several relationships and many dating situations with variations on the theme to allow Joel and I to glean from the complex human interactions of his love life these two—perhaps simplistically typecast but nonetheless very real—types of women. But when we did, I asked Joel how he would describe himself in terms of these types. Not surprisingly, his response was that he was more along the lines of the psycho chick than the flower girl. But I then reminded him of a piece of his history. As a child, older neighborhood boys used to take advantage of him: Eager to please and be accepted by the group, he would run various errands for them. One time they even talked him into dancing naked in the snow for them. Also, as a teenager, and even later in early adulthood, his older brother repeatedly talked him into lending him money even though he never paid it back.

Joel responded to this reminder with a flood of memories and associations, which pretty quickly revealed that underneath his worldly and complicated sophistication he had a sweet, simple, and trusting—you might even say naive—disposition. Over the years, because he felt ashamed of where this disposition took him, Joel had "covered it over" with his skeptical, critical, overly developed intellect. However, it was still an authentic part of him, if a disavowed one, which was why he would always look for it in the flower girls. Of course, sooner or later these girls would remind him of his own shameful, sweet naiveté, and he would have to dissociate from them as well. He would then date the opposite type of girl, and predictably enough, when these psycho chicks put him through the ringer, he would once again feel the need for uncomplicated, sweet, simple love.

But after I'd inserted this historical-psychological mirror in front of him—which, truth be told, I had to do repeatedly over a period of time—Joel was finally able to reach Step One. He accepted this previously renounced aspect of himself and integrated it into his more intellectual style. Since he now saw that this eager-to-please, naive little boy was still very much with him,

he no longer needed to look for women who would embody—
or, in unconscious collusion with him, would develop—these attributes for his internal benefit. Likewise, he no longer needed to
date women who, in their worldly sophistication, would help
him escape this little boy.

And now that he had stopped using women as a mirror, he
was able to engage in the work of Step Two, Understanding
Your Ambivalence, in which he would ask himself what kind of
woman and relationship he actually wanted. This work, of
course, was not strictly cognitive as in sitting and thinking but
rather involved cognition interacting with action and experience. So when meeting a woman now, Joel would no longer present himself as an intimidating intellectual, setting her up to
counterpresent as either a sweet girl or as a competing intellectual. Rather, he would allow both his simple concerns with love
and his intellectual interests guide the conversation and his behavior. This balance naturally drew to him more balanced
women. Now the more he accepted his previously disowned
simple, sweet self, the clearer he became that on the continuum
between the flower girl and the psycho chick—he had now discovered there was a rich middle ground in between the two—he
ultimately wanted to be with someone closer to the latter. It was
now important for him to be sincere and kind himself but
equally important to have a partner with whom he could hold
intellectual conversations.

Joel thus ended up marrying an exciting, adventurous woman
who had a demanding career in journalism. This was not an easy
move because just after they got engaged Joel lost his job in the
bursting Internet bubble. He remained unemployed for many
months, and this played havoc with his self-esteem, particularly
when he'd compare his career status to his fiancée's. But he
didn't cover up his vulnerability with complicated rationaliza-
tions and philosophical ranting. His honesty and openness about

his career struggles at that time in effect tested his fiancée's ability to be sweet and kind herself. And in fact, though she was a driven, ambitious person, she was completely supportive of him. Her priority remained with him and the relationship, and they were able to weather the storm.

JUMPING INTO THE WATER

As illustrated by the case above, Step Two in overcoming Narcissistic Love involves getting to know something critical or fundamental about yourself, which in turn allows you to make a good choice in picking a partner. One of the most dramatic examples of this I've seen is a patient who came to see me because of a conflict in sexual identity. An attractive, intelligent woman in her late twenties, the patient was sexually and emotionally attracted to both men and women. With the exception of one heterosexual relationship during high school, however, she pretty much stayed away from romantic relationships with either. After some time in therapy, the patient got involved with a man. Together, they developed a good, open relationship, with many intimate conversations, lots of fun and an active, exciting sex life. After about a year they started talking about marriage, but whereas my patient felt she was ready to make a commitment, the boyfriend said he needed a couple of more years to build his career.

My patient then began to question his seriousness and this sent her into a spiral of panic. She became preoccupied and obsessed with the possibility that if they ended up getting married, her boyfriend would ultimately turn out to be like her father— who early in her life had cheated on her mother and then abandoned the family. She therefore began to interrogate her boyfriend about his sexual fantasies, interests in other women, and reluctance to commit. At the same time she put pressure on him to prove his commitment by moving in together or getting engaged. Although he resisted for a while, it was clear to me that he loved her and that he was in fact moving toward making a commitment. And indeed, at some point during this time he suggested—and not at all in the grudging way in which you might yield to an ultimatum—that they move in together.

But this only increased my patient's anxiety. In her franticness she searched through her boyfriend's things and came across a photo of a previous girlfriend in the nude. This was it for her—she was now convinced he was the kind of man who would cheat on her. She told him she wasn't going to move in with him and was in fact thinking of moving away. At the same time she was also developing a crush on a female coworker. He questioned and protested, but it was becoming painfully evident that their relationship was unraveling.

It was in one of her therapy sessions during this period that the patient began to engage in the work of Step One. It happened when I commented that there were no real data to suggest that her boyfriend *was* like her father. If anything, I argued—and the patient quickly concurred—her fears and accusations were a projection: she was the one who wanted out of the relationship just when he proposed to live together; and she was the one who was like (or identified with) her father, suddenly interested in someone else and unable to commit.

Building on this Step One-type insight, the patient then added a few more brushstrokes to this painful self-portrait: I am the person who has stayed out of relationships for years; I'm the person who is leaving and hurting this man who loves me; I'm the one who is not even sure about my sexual orientation and therefore don't know what I want.

As painful as the subsequent breakup was for both my patient and her boyfriend, it was clearly unavoidable because you can't commit to something you don't know you want. Which is where Step Two comes into the picture. Once she stopped projecting and owned that *she* was the one bowing out of the relationship, the patient realized she had to explore her sexuality more deeply. And this, in turn, led her to the conclusion that she really wanted to be with a woman. This was not simply a theoretical conclusion, and in fact, illustrating that these steps are not always as distinct as I'm describing them, shortly after breaking up with her boyfriend, she got involved with her coworker, and over time this turned into a long-term, committed relationship.

It goes without saying that this vignette does not capture this patient's sexual or interpersonal journey and that her therapy as a whole was much more complex. Nonetheless, it describes not only the moment of transition from Step One to Step Two, but also the practical reality that in working through these steps you must "jump into the water." You must try new behaviors and various relationships rather than sit on the sidelines. You might get hurt and you might hurt others, but that's the only way to find out what you really want.

A word of warning: Don't fall into the trap of trying a new relationship before trying something new in the old relationship. Many young couples come to therapy to figure out if they want to commit to each other once their early mutual idealization lessens. They often don't know what they want because their initial attraction to each other, as well as their subsequent doubts, are based on narcissistic projections. It is only by staying past the point of idealization and devaluation that we can see beyond our projections and thereby learn from our experience with the *actual* partner whether this is something we *actually* want.

STEP THREE: RESOLVING YOUR AMBIVALENCE

"I guess I should give you some of the background," said Janet, an attractive woman in her late thirties who came to see me because of a crisis in her marriage.

My marriage is the second serious relationship in my life. The first one, which I keep thinking about these days, was in college. I'm from a small town in southern Jersey, and I came to New York for college. We were both English majors, but he was much more serious about it, writing poetry and short stories and planning to become a writer. He was really talented, I think, but also incredibly romantic and handsome. He was kind of sophisticated, I guess. He grew up in the city—in Soho. His father was a well-known artist. Anyway, he was the first man I had sex with and he was incredibly sensual and gentle. Basically, he swept me off my feet and I completely idolized him. We were together for four years, and I learned so much from him about art and literature and life in New York. I was really happy for most of this time—I'm not sure I've ever been as happy, although now I wonder how real it all was. I thought he was so wonderful, and I think the fact that someone like him wanted me made me feel special. Anyway, real or not, I'll never forget this one night when we took the Staten Island Ferry, just for the ride. We were on the ferry, looking at the Manhattan skyline, and the water, and the stars, and I felt this surge of love and being loved, and I promised myself I'd never forget that moment.

At this point I smiled and mentioned to her a *New Yorker* cartoon showing a dramatic, water-edge New York skyline and a miniature couple at the bottom, with the capture reading, "The thing I like about New York, Claudia, is you." Janet smiled too as she understood that much of this first love of hers was about being in love with love and infusing the relationship—for better and worse—with the full ecstasy of romantic narcissism. "So what happened to the relationship?" I asked. She continued:

Well, it was all pretty much focused on him—his artistic aspirations, his career, his struggles to find work when we graduated from college. That didn't really bother me because I loved him so much, and in fact after college we moved in together and I supported us while he was working on a collection of short stories, which I just found out he eventually published. But during this time he would also hang out with a more 'cool,' downtown crowd that I couldn't relate to. So he would go out to clubs and I'd stay home or spend time with friends. Then one day he confessed that he was sleeping with another woman whom he met in one of those clubs. So we broke up and I was heartbroken for a very long time.

I've been thinking about this relationship recently because this kind of love and intensity is precisely what's missing from my marriage. The strange thing is, a couple of weeks ago, completely out of nowhere, I get an e-mail from Jeremy—that guy—saying it would be nice to get back in touch. So I met him for lunch, in part out of curiosity, to see what I would feel for him now. It turned out it was one of the most boring lunches I've ever had. He was in a way the same, talking about his struggle with writing, books he's been reading and nightclubs or dinner parties he's been to. He was completely self-absorbed and strangely lacking in any charm. He was single and had no children. And of course, he was balding.

It absolutely amazed me that this man whom I was so taken with and influenced by now seemed so boring and empty, that I didn't even care to see or not see him again. Which brings me back to my marriage. David and I have been together for ten years and we have two children, a boy and a girl. After Jeremy and I broke up I was consciously looking for someone grounded and reliable, which took a long time to find, because I was still attracted to those exciting, downtown artist types. But David was different from the very beginning. We fell in love, that's for sure, but it was much quieter, I guess more mature. Also, I was more in the center of the relationship, and David was completely devoted and admiring of me. He made me feel good about my body again, saying I was the most beautiful woman he'd ever seen. He had just gotten his first decent job and he said he wanted to have a family with me. He was always there for me and I knew that this was part of why I was with him. After Jeremy and a couple of other poet types, I finally realized I wanted to be with someone real, someone who for a change would put me *on a pedestal.*

Anyway, we eventually got married and had the children. He was becoming successful and I was working part time, focusing more on being a mother, which by the way, I think is the greatest thing. But our relationship has become more and more routine, like a business partnership, or perhaps like a sister and brother, and I'm really missing the romance. We don't fight that much and he is a good father and he loads the dishwasher and changes the lightbulbs. But he has no spirit, or pizzazz, or something. Maybe he is depressed, I don't know. I feel he is too much of an observer, like he needs me to entertain him. He's passive, and he doesn't have much to say or to give. We have a lot in common, and our past together, and I definitely don't want to separate. But I don't know that I would've stayed in the marriage if we didn't have kids. I guess I feel there's not enough love in our relationship.

Notwithstanding Janet's seriousness, sadness, and concern at that moment, I once again smiled, thinking and sharing with her yet another *New Yorker* cartoon in which one spouse tells the other, "O.K., maybe there's no chemistry left, but there's still archeology." Of course, I mentioned these cartoons to the patient because they illustrated that her struggle with love was universal rather than pathological and, more specifically, that it was underscored by the problem of idealization. This patient's particular path, traversing from a relationship in which she was the Echo to one in which she was the Narcissus, is indeed common. And looking at her journey from a therapeutic perspective, we can see that by the time she came to see me Janet had already struggled and perhaps mastered Steps One and Two of my three-step approach: she figured out that much of her first relationship was based on idealization and mirroring (Step One), and that she ultimately wanted to be with a reliable, steady, "down-to-earth" partner (Step Two). But while she had faced her projections, denials, and escapes and was therefore able to commit to a relationship, she was now confronted by what she was previously so afraid of: her ambivalence. She was unhappy in her marriage because she was deeply ambivalent about her husband—liking the security, stability, and commonality he provided but hating his passivity and dullness. Enter Step Three, Resolving Your Ambivalence.

In Step Three, we move beyond our narcissistic concern of feeling good about ourselves to loving our partner for who he is, including, most particularly, the ways in which he is different from us. To get there, we must put aside our narcissism, which paradoxically, yet critically, we can only accomplish by first indulging it. Let me explain. In the case of Janet, her first relationship, and to a large extent her second, were highly loaded with her narcissism—her need to feel good about herself. In general, her self-esteem depended almost entirely on her relationships—with Jeremy, with David, and with her children. *But she has never done anything for her self-esteem outside of her relationships.* This is still a problem for many women, for as research shows, men's self-esteem depends more on their ability to perform (at work and sexually), whereas women's self-esteem depends more on having successful relationships (and on physical appearance).

In her therapy Janet quickly came to see that though she was quite talented, she had never indulged her noninterpersonal gifts. She loved language and literature, but this was mostly evident in her life in the kind of men she pursued when younger. She was rather passive with respect to her own interests and somehow expected her partners—now her husband—to stimulate her. Once she realized this, Janet decided to go back to school to get a graduate degree in comparative literature. She didn't know where this would lead her, but once she started studying, a new, powerful dynamic developed in the marriage. She had less time with David, so less time to criticize him. She was so much happier and more stimulated that she wanted to talk to David about what *she* was doing rather than just wanting to listen to *him*. She therefore once again began to appreciate his "passivity," which she now experienced as great listening skills. However, unlike at the beginning of their relationship, she wasn't just enjoying being on center stage or being admired by him. She was actually enjoying the literature she was talking about. And because she was so much into it, she was carefully listening to what David was saying, thereby discovering and appreciating that his perspective and contributions were quite different from her thoughts. All of a sudden she was able to enjoy David for who he was—someone who could listen, ask questions, and develop a conversation with a unique point of view. And the more she appreciated this, the more David elaborated and the more he had to say.

Finally, in a parallel change to Janet—apparently because he didn't want to stay behind or perhaps because he was inspired by her—David decided to pursue more of his own "selfish" interests. Feeling that his career was somewhat at a standstill and having a bit more time because his wife wasn't home that much, he started to write a series of magazine articles based on his work as a human resources executive. Now *he* wanted to talk more—about his articles—not just to listen, which changed the dynamic of their relationship altogether, making it far more balanced and integrated.

So once Janet decided to give herself what she needed to feed her narcissism, she no longer expected that from David. She was thus more able to accept and even enjoy his imperfections (in this case his "passivity" or "dullness"). David, in turn, felt more accepted and loved and was therefore able to step out of his comfort zone and to initiate more stimulation and growth in himself. So as Janet was becoming more integrated—no longer Echo or Narcissus but a bit of both—so was David. In short, Janet "got a life," and then she got a husband.

To reduce Step Three to its basic ingredients, we might prescribe the following: (1) get a life and stop focusing so much on your partner; (2) appreciate what your partner has to offer, not what he doesn't; and (3) notice his growth, which will usually come in parallel to yours. In the next couple of chapters I will describe in detail some specific techniques for implementing Step Three within a relationship. First, let's see how it can be worked on in a dating situation.

One couple had been dating for several months and came for a consultation because the woman was tired of being criticized by her boyfriend for not talking in group situations. "It bothers me that when we are, like, with friends, she is always quiet," he explained. "I think it makes people uncomfortable and they also wonder what's wrong with her." The woman became visibly upset by this criticism. "None of my friends ever say they are uncomfortable with it," she shot back in anger. It was clear to me from the get-go that it was him, the boyfriend, not other friends, who felt uncomfortable with the silence and thought there was something wrong with her. In short, I suspected he was devaluing her.

So using Step One, I explored with him *his* feelings about silence and not talking, and amazingly enough it turned out that as a child he had stuttered and was therefore teased into silence and withdrawal. While his stutter was completely gone by now, his self-esteem still suffered and he needed his girlfriend to talk in groups so as not to be reminded of his childhood pain. Once we made this connection, the patient was able to progress into Step Two, where he realized that what he truly wanted was not a talkative, outgoing girlfriend who would make a good impression on his friends but rather one was who good to him—patient, supportive, honest, and responsible—which was what he already had in his girlfriend. He thus let go of his expectation that she speak up and then entered Step Three, in which he was trying to improve his self-esteem more directly, by doing something *himself* and subsequently coming to see that while his girlfriend wasn't talking much in these group situations, she always had some really interesting observations afterward. So he was now more interested in her observations than in her silence, seeing and appreciating her on her own terms.

As evident from all these cases, by definition, Step Three can only be fully implemented in the context of a relationship. However, even in the absence of a relationship, there are things you can do to lay the groundwork for it. In the context of Narcissistic Love, the most important thing you can do is to dedicate yourself to something at which you can really excel. This something could be work, or any other major, personal—though not interpersonal—pursuit. Be it investment banking, gardening, interior decoration, or charitable work, find out what's in it for you and immerse yourself in it. If your relationship history is more along the Echo than Narcissus line, or if your work is primarily a way of making money without much room for subjective enjoyment, make sure you initiate and embrace something really selfish, such as painting, writing, yoga, exercise—really anything, as long as you do it for yourself. If you are more of a Narcissus, you should still do something selfish but something you can be passionate about because you enjoy it, not because it looks good or will impress others.

2

Virtual Love

Could this be flesh, or was it ivory only?
No, it could not be ivory.
OVID

The original Pygmalion—from the Greek myth—was a celebrated sculptor who was turned off to women, considering them all to be untrustworthy whores. Yet he desperately needed these objects of his disdain, certainly wanting one to share his bed. So capitalizing on his creative talents, he crafted a statue of a woman, making it more beautiful than any woman could ever be. And of course, Pygmalion ended up falling in love with his own workmanship.

He named her Galatea and he showered her with flowers, pebbles, pet birds, and clothes. He talked to her, he held her, and he kissed her. And then—what else? He took her to bed with him. We don't know exactly what happened next, except that Pygmalion was now deeply in love and praying to Venus for a wife just like his ivory girl. One night, as he was stroking her breast, the ivory softened, "made pliable by handling." As Pygmalion kissed her lips, he felt them warming. Then Galatea blushed, her eyes opened, and . . . a blessed marriage quickly followed.

If only life imitated myth! Actually, it does, but only up to a point. Indeed, even under the most ordinary circumstances, falling in love is a creative, miraculous, and somewhat solipsistic affair. As we saw in the previous chapter, when we are in love, we think this other person is very special, but the fact is that we also create an image of him or her in our mind so that he or she will give us exactly what we need. In this sense, falling in love is about overlooking imperfections that otherwise we are only all too willing to observe. A long nose, receding hairline, big thighs, big nostrils, big ego, small breasts, or small pockets are all irrelevant when we're in love. When my patients date and then decide it's not the right person, they often explain it with "She's not smart enough," or "He's a little boring," or "She's just not that attractive," or "He's not ambitious enough." They stubbornly refuse to ignore the other person's deficiencies. But when they fall in love, not only do they ignore such deficiencies, they also exaggerate, elaborate, and even invent positive features and traits that are merely in the eyes of the beholder.

Taken to an extreme, this is the Pygmalion syndrome, which is often a central feature of Virtual Love. We are in love with a prefabricated construction of our own making, which has little to do with the actual person we are dating. Unfortunately, we don't always know this early enough in the relationship because unconsciously we choose people and situations that obscure reality. In the case of Virtual Love, these "people and situations" most commonly involve a long-distance relationship. I'm in New York, she's in Boston. We met when I visited a college friend in Cambridge and we had an instant connection: great conversation, unbelievable sex. I then started going there every other weekend and she comes here too. We can never get enough of each other and our weekends are packed with fun activities and good times. Then we start talking about the next step—commitment. Who would move, who would quit their job, can we do it on a trial basis? Who will pay for the move?

And what about supporting the one unemployed? Should we get married first? What about her autistic brother? Do I want something like this in my children's genetic makeup? And she: how are we going to deal with your mother coming every Saturday to clean your apartment and change your sheets? And more important: what if I quit my job, leave my family and friends, and move to New York, and six months later you change your mind? "Yes," I say—or at least think—"what if I start resenting you for depending on me too much? And what if you start resenting me for asking you to give up so much and move here for me?"

For obvious reasons, in the long-distance relationship, these kinds of questions have an extra intensity—we cannot test them against reality without making the big move. To be sure, the Big Move can work, but only if both parties are ready to throw caution to the wind, make a commitment, and stick to it come what may. But that's a big if, because these days most young people practically require empirical proof that "it can work" before making such a commitment. In addition, the unfortunate fact is that many long-distance relationships are a fixed game. That is, the concerns of reality rear their ugly head with particular vengeance because on some level we know all along that our weekends together—as wonderful and bittersweet as they have been—are a work of fiction. The problem is not so much that we ignored the fact of our geographical distance but rather that we have used it to avoid feeling ambivalent about the other person. We used it to avoid feeling put off by her neediness or my aloofness, or her defective genes or my dependency on my mother, and so on.

As the Big Move becomes more likely, those deficiencies loom even larger. Do I really want someone who has no life? Why else would she be willing to throw away everything for me? And she: why should I move for someone who's so selfish and spoiled? So as much as we have tried to create a perfect relationship, sculpting our weekends together with the conscious spontaneity of romance but the unconscious precision of an architectural blueprint, we slowly but surely approach the moment of truth, where anger, blame, and rejection creep, or sometimes burst, into the relationship. Sadly, this truth is not the full truth either. If the Pygmalion syndrome is one extreme, in due course it often leads us to the opposite extreme: the Frankenstein syndrome. Like Frankenstein in the Mary Shelley book, we end up creating a monster that will turn on us. Chances are she is not a needy, defective loser after all! But the more balanced truth is what we unconsciously wanted to avoid feeling upfront—love in spite of ambivalence.

So in order not to end up with the Frankenstein syndrome, we must deal as early as possible with the Pygmalion syndrome. Dealing with it early is what I've always tried to do with my patients—so many of whom at various times struggle with the dynamics of a long-distance relationship. As we saw in the previous chapter, however, it's not always easy to catch these things early.

STEP ONE: RECOGNIZING YOUR PATTERN

As with the stock market or gardening, when it comes to love we are lucky if we make the same mistake only twice. There is a deadly combination at work here: it's very important for us to find love, and yet we are infinitely capable of deluding ourselves about our emotions. In other words, our mistakes disguise themselves, so until we know how they—or really we—operate, we are doomed to repeat them. In therapy, as in life, we need to get to that frustrating, depressing place of "here I go again," and sometimes more than once, before we are truly ready to turn a new page.

One of my patients, Julie, was an energetic and brainy litigation attorney. A senior associate in a large law firm, she was assertive and articulate. She came to see me sometime after her thirty-first birthday, when she could no longer believe it was just bad luck that was preventing her from meeting Mr. Right. So while she knew she was doing something wrong, she couldn't figure out what it was. As luck would have it, a short time after we started working together she met a man, Jeff, on a business trip to Los Angeles. She was immediately drawn to him because, as she put it, "he had a relaxed, open-minded approach to life." She was also excited because he was planning a career change that involved a move to New York in a few months.

For a couple of months, they spoke on the phone and e-mailed each other back and forth. Then they spent a couple of weekends together. When I saw Julie for her session after her second LA weekend with Jeff, she was clearly on the verge of falling in love. "He is so generous, emotionally, and he's so receptive. And he's smart without being aggressive," she said. "And he is also not a workaholic—which is really good for me," she added. From that point on, Julie flew to California every Friday night and spent the weekends with Jeff, until a couple of months later he made the move to New York. Julie was thrilled, and they began to talk about engagement and marriage. The only thing that bothered her was that the job and apartment he got in New York were not so great. But she figured, once he's more established, he'll move on. But when she mentioned this to him, she realized that she was the only one who had a problem with his situation. Jeff said he really liked his job and had no interest in changing it anytime soon. He also didn't mind his apartment. For one thing, he liked to spend most of his free time outside, and he certainly was more outdoorsy than she was.

Then came time to make a plan for summer vacation. But whereas she wanted to go to Paris and Rome, to visit museums and ruins and to wine and dine, all he wanted was to go to the beach. Also, he was beginning to complain that she was working too many hours, that she was not spiritual enough, and that she was too driven. And correspondingly, she began to see him as passive, slow, soft-headed, and naive. As often happens in relationships, the qualities that drew her to him in the first place, his "relaxed, open-minded approach to life" were now repellent. So with this dynamic in full force, just about three months after he moved to New York, Julie "fell out of love" and broke up the relationship.

Now Julie was the first to acknowledge that part of the problem in her relationship with Jeff was that it started long distance. "Upon closer examination," she mocked her own lawyerly manner, "the suspect simply turned out to be different from who I thought he was. Also, when I visited him in LA, I was kind of on vacation and more into that relaxed California mind-set than I normally would be." With that bit of analysis, and grasping for a practical, commonsense implementation of a lesson well learned, Julie vowed, "No more long-distance relationships." She also vowed, "No more nice, soft, passive men," and she cleared her head for new dating experiences.

After several blind and semiblind dates arranged through work, church, and friends, Julie began to explore Internet dating services. And lo and behold, through e-dating, she met a man who lived three blocks away from her, and who described himself to Julie in their first online communication as "a take charge, no nonsense kind of a guy." A young stockbroker, he was hard working and ambitious. And he would definitely go to Paris and Rome on vacation, he said. "The beach is boring—too mellow for me." He agreed with Julie when she described her last relationship. During this period, Julie was preparing for a trial, which for a litigator is the equivalent of an extended cramming period for a final exam. She worked evenings and weekends and she was perpetually tired. But her interest in her date was grow-ing, so she made sure to find a few minutes here and there for e-mailing and instant messaging. He too was busy, but he said he'd really like to take her out soon. Julie said yes, but she also wanted to wait awhile not only because the trial would be over soon but also because she felt there was a strong potential for a relationship here, and she didn't want to jump into anything as she had done in her previous relationship. So it took about a month of e-dating before they made the switch to r-dating (where r = reality).

That first date went very well, as both found that they were strongly attracted to each other. But now *he* had a situation at work that required overtime for a couple of weeks. So it was an-other three weeks before their second date, but three weeks of increasingly passionate late-night instant messaging and e-love. At last, Jim's schedule cleared off, and they began to date regu-larly. They got along very well, because they had many similar interests and values. At times, however, Julie found him to be too dominating—things definitely had to be his way. Initially she went along with it because she felt she was "taken care of" by a strong man. But after a couple of months she began to stand up to him, and they started arguing with growing frequency: what show to go to, which restaurant, whether and when to see their families, who should apologize first, how and when to have sex, and so on and so forth. "I want to work it out with him, I really love him," Julie told me in a session describing this dynamic. "It's just that we both have strong personalities, and I guess we're fighting for control," she analyzed.

But that's not how Jim saw it. The next session, Julie walked in and burst into tears. "He broke up with me," she cried. "He said I was too controlling and aggressive, that he was not going to spend the rest of his life in a power struggle, and that he didn't believe in 'working' on relationships." We spent some time in therapy mourning the loss, but in her ever-practical way Julie moved rather quickly, wanting to know where she went wrong and what to do differently in the next dating or relationship situation. As we discussed it, two things emerged. First, on the rebound from the previous relationship, Julie was like the general who was fighting the previous war, a sure recipe for losing. After the last relationship she vowed to never again date a "wimp." So of course, she ended up with a bully. (This is an example of how in real life the patterns of failed love overlap; for further discussion of wimps and bullies, see chapter 7.)

The second thing, I told Julie, "You once again got involved in a long-distance relationship." *"What?"* She looked at me with amazement. "Who's the nut here, me or you! Jim lives around the corner from me!" "I know," I said, "my memory is not *that* bad. But for the first couple of months you and he had an e-relationship, remember? It was then that you fell in love, just like with what's-his-name from LA, and just like Pygmalion," and I went on to explain how, in the absence of regular physical contact it's easy to fall in love with our own mental construction. "I can't believe I did it again!" Julie exclaimed, getting closer to her "here I go again" moment. I say "getting closer," because, like so many of us, Julie had to catch herself in the act in order to fully get it. So her "here I go again" moment arrived only a couple of months later when she was tempted, but ultimately declined, to get involved with a European man who was here on a one-year work assignment. . . .

Now while in hindsight it's easy to see that the Pygmalion syndrome was the common denominator in both of Julie's relationships, it was hard, if at all possible, to know this at the time the relationships were occurring. That's because on the surface these relationships seemed so different from each other. One was with a "passive" man, the other with an "aggressive" man; one Julie broke up with, the other "dumped" her.

STEP TWO: UNDERSTANDING YOUR
AMBIVALENCE

This second step involves, first and foremost, understanding and accepting the ambivalence that underlies the Pygmalion syndrome. Once the disguising influence of her virtual dating wore off, Julie was forced to acknowledge her ambivalence toward her boyfriends. She was ambivalent about her first boyfriend— loving his relaxed open-mindedness but hating his passivity— and she was ambivalent about her second boyfriend—loving his take-charge attitude but hating his aggressiveness, at least insofar as she constantly battled it. Realizing this, she now had to decide what kind of man she wanted to be with. While the world of men can hardly be divided into wimps and bullies, they don't say "nice guys finish last" for nothing. In other words, men who aggressively devote themselves to external "success" are likely to be less sensitive or supportive, and those who enjoy talking about relationships and spending time with their children are going to be less aggressive in the career battlefield. Of course, like all of us, Julie wanted to have it all. Why shouldn't she? The problem was, time was marching on, and she could no longer wait for Mr. Perfect. More important, she was beginning to entertain the strange notion that Mr. Perfect didn't really exist.

So how do you choose between two equally appealing (and unappealing) options? The only answer to that is *by knowing yourself really well.* For many of us this means more therapy, but for others it simply means answering the question What's my bottom line? In Julie's case, the question translated into "Is it more important for me to be with a man who is open and supportive or with one who is take-charge and successful? Or, as I posed it to her, "Will you be more unhappy if you feel your husband is passive and weak, or if you feel he's a workaholic who pays no attention to your feelings?" Since her father was the latter type, it was easy for Julie, at least in theory, to go with the former. To many readers this may sound like "settling" or compromising on love. But as Step Three will demonstrate, that's not what I have in mind.

STEP THREE: RESOLVING YOUR AMBIVALENCE

There's a saying in business, "The trend is your friend," which means that if you are in the horse-and-buggy business and somebody invents a motorized buggy with no horse, rather than trying to convince people that cars are no good, you start making them yourself. You thus end up with more, not less, than what you've started with. This sounds simple, but it isn't, not only because you don't know how to make cars but also because your natural instinct is to push your own product against the competition. Indeed, the very way your company is organized—its way of being in the world—is based on that instinct. To use a slightly more romantic metaphor, when it comes to relationships we are often like a surfer who insists on mastering the wave not by riding it but rather by busting right through it.

After deciding that when push comes to shove she'd prefer to be with a "softer" rather than a "tougher" man, my patient Julie had to deal with the consequences of her choice, that is, her negative feelings about her man's "softness." When she fell in love with, and became engaged to, a man who was on the softer side, her natural tendency was to deal with it by bucking the trend. As with her first boyfriend, she tried to "encourage" her fiancé to take initiative and to become more assertive and ambitious. And she fought to get him to like the things that she liked. It wasn't much of a fight though, because being supportive he naturally tried to accommodate her. He was in fact so accommodating that he even tried to be more aggressive and . . . less accommodating. Obviously, this didn't work, because the more he accepted her suggestions, the weaker he seemed in her eyes. And it couldn't have worked anyway, because it's impossible to change another person. It's hard enough to change oneself!

So in Step Three, Resolving Your Ambivalence, Julie's job was to accept her fiancé for who he was. In particular, she had to accept the fact that he was not that aggressive about his career aspirations. For a while, though, no matter how hard she tried she couldn't help it. She couldn't help it, because she felt that in "accepting his limitations," as she put it, she was doing something just for *him* and, in a way, *against herself.* It was only when she remembered and reremembered—how quickly we forget!—that the reason she chose him in the first place was because she needed some softness in her life that Julie became more open to who her fiancé was. Only then, when she realized that he represented an unfulfilled part of herself—the softer, emotional, sensitive girl she never allowed herself to be because she desperately wanted to please her powerful father—did Julie decide to stop trying to change her fiancé and to start changing herself.

But even with this new and genuine sense of resolution it was difficult for Julie to change. For one thing, Julie didn't like to do some of the things her fiancé enjoyed, like hanging out, going to the beach, or renting a video. She wanted to "do" things: go to lectures, movies, museums, and so on. "The trend is your friend," I said at that point, knowing that the business metaphor would appeal to the still resistant, tough-minded father figure she had inside of her. I also explained to her what I called the Demosthenes Principle.

Demosthenes was the greatest orator in ancient Greece. But he didn't start out that way. In fact, as a child he could hardly talk because he had a speech impediment. How did he become a great orator? As there were no speech therapists at that time, Demosthenes, the child, came up with his own treatment: he would practice speaking over the sound of the ocean's waves with pebbles in his mouth. Rather than try to avoid his difficulty and take the path of least resistance, he did the opposite—he made it even harder for himself. That's how he mastered it.

There was a similar concept in behavioral treatment of phobias called implosion therapy. If someone has a fear of flying, for instance, you force him to fly on a four-seater in bad weather or something to that effect. You expose him fully, with little preparation, to the anxiety-producing stimulus. But as anyone suffering from a phobia could tell you, this form of treatment is pretty much doomed from the start. It is too anxiety-provoking for most patients. But it worked for Julie because going to the beach or hanging out was hardly a frightening stimulus; it was just something she didn't like to do. Or so she thought until she got into it.

How did she get into it? The general principle was, she *changed by becoming more of herself.* More specifically, the first time she went with her fiancé on a beach vacation she brought her office—laptop, BlackBerry, briefs, and so on—with her, and she had a great time working on the beach. In other words, she found a way of making it work for *her.* In time, of course, the breeze and the sand and the sound of the waves won her over from those exciting legal briefs. Interestingly, the more Julie would just hang out, the more her fiancé wanted to go out and *do* things. Also, the more she allowed herself the softness she needed in her life, the more her fiancé allowed himself his hitherto unexpressed aggression. *So by giving to themselves they each gave to the other.* This was how, instead of getting further polarized by their differences, they ended up in the all-desirable, though often elusive, middle ground.

Of course, Julie didn't fully follow the Demosthenes Principle.

She didn't go to the beach without anything to do, completely giving herself over to the sun, sand, and salt. And in this way, I suspect, most of us are more like Julie than like Demosthenes. We try to escape rather than to embrace our limitations, which is why for most people the Demosthenes Principle can only become useful somewhat late in their search for love. Early on in life we dream about faraway love while rejecting the love of our dreams, which more often than not is right in our own backyard. This was certainly why Pygmalion went slowly with women, starting with a statue first. . . . The thing is, you can't wait for too long to deal with your ambivalence about love because under most circumstances, ivory does not become flesh.

By now it should be pretty evident that my three-step approach is not as simple or linear as I make it seem. The steps can overlap, and their implementation sometimes means moving two steps forward and one step back. But the more we are aware of these steps, the more forward movement we make. For some people, following the steps is an uphill battle. Much like a prisoner who is released from a life sentence but returns to jail because he's unable to adjust to freedom, they are drawn back by, and revert to, their old, self-defeating relationship patterns. As I discussed in the introduction, the main reason for this draw is our fear of ambivalence. But there are other important reasons that should be mentioned, chief among which is what's known in psychoanalytic theory as the repetition compulsion. According to this principle, we unconsciously feel compelled to repeat something we have suffered from in order to master it and to come out on top. So a woman who had an emotionally or physically absent father—certainly not an uncommon occurrence in our lives and times—might unconsciously choose to love a man who lives in another city. She gets to repeat the experience of longing for a distant man, but this time with the hope that her adult power will make the outcome of the relationship different.

In addition to—some scientists say instead of—the repetition compulsion, there is also evidence that our early childhood love experiences leave physiological traces in our brain, which then become perceptual pathways or easy "default" trails for similar behavioral patterns. And finally, there is habit, familiarity, and the accompanying fear of change that may well be the most powerful human motivator. All these explain why for some people the three-step approach is difficult to implement even in psychotherapy.

But many people repeat these patterns in a manner that hinders but does not necessarily imprison them. In those cases, the three steps can be used as a relatively simple introspective process outside the therapeutic setting. The question is how to know which "category" you belong to—how serious is your repetition? In retrospect it's easy to tell. One patient at the age of thirty-two met a man from out of state whom she had once dated in college. After a month of dating she decided to move to his state and marry him. They were married in six months and were still married with children ten years later. Compare this with another patient of a similar age who met a man who was in the process of applying to graduate school. She encouraged him to apply to a school in Michigan, because at the time she was thinking she'd be moving there for an academic position the following year. Well, he did, but she ended up not moving there because, among other things, after a year of long-distance dating she decided he was not for her. This woman continued to engage in failed love patterns for several more years, at which time she finally got into therapy.

This, of course, is an after-the-fact comparison. But was there a way to tell at the time, before these women became fully

involved in a long-distance relationship, which one was destined
to the failed pattern of Virtual Love and which would end up
converting the long-distance dating into an actual long-term
relationship? While we can't know for sure, I believe you can tell
this sort of thing very early in the dating process.

The following are several scenarios, all based on real situations from the lives of my patients; in each scenario I will identify the signs, or so-called red flags, suggesting a self-defeating
outcome. While we can easily generalize from these scenarios to
all Virtual Love dating situations, a word of caution is in order.
The "dating rules" offered by some self-help books are often
based on conventional common sense and are not universally
true. In addition, life is richer when you follow your own intu-
ition, judgment, and experience or when you develop your own
interpersonal rules. On the other hand, there's no need to reinvent the wheel, and so to some extent we can learn from the experiences of others. The bottom line: use these scenarios and red
flags as guidelines, not rules.

VIRTUAL LOVE SCENARIOS

DATING BEFORE MOVING

Three months before moving to New York for graduate school
you meet, and start a relationship with, a wonderful man. Though
you both know you are moving, you don't discuss the futility
of getting involved until a week before you leave. You then decide he'll come to visit you a month later. He ends up not being
able to come, but you go to visit him. You have great time and in
the next six months you visit a couple of more times. You talk
on the phone a few times a week and when you bring up the

"what are we doing" question, he says, "I don't know. I wish we could make it work; maybe I can move to New York at some point." But in subsequent conversations you get the feeling he doesn't want to talk about it and you don't feel comfortable bringing it up again. When you finally do bring it up he says, "I don't really know what to tell you. Let's just not talk about it all the time."

Red Flags

- You don't acknowledge the difficulties of the relationship at the very beginning, which suggests you are not taking each other seriously and/or are unwilling to deal with the reality of the situation.
- He doesn't follow through on his plan to visit you in New York, indicating the relationship is not a priority.
- You do all the visiting, suggesting a lack of reciprocity.
- He's tentative and vague on the critical issue in the relationship—"Maybe I can move to New York at some point"—which demonstrates a casual acceptance of the basic situation.
- He doesn't want to talk about "the relationship" and you don't feel comfortable pursuing the topic.

It would have been a different story if you both acknowledged the "craziness" of getting involved when you are about to move; if he were to keep his word and visit you; if he were to do some of the visiting, showing reciprocity and commitment; if he were making a concrete, gradual plan to move (as opposed to not making any plans or impulsively quitting his job and moving to New York); if he too wanted to talk about the long-distance aspect of the relationship, suggesting he would've liked to transform the relationship from the virtual to the real as much as you did.

A Voice (E-mail) from the Past

On your thirty-fourth birthday you receive an e-mail from someone with whom you had a three-week relationship back in college. At that time, he was visiting a mutual friend before leaving the country for a year as an exchange student. You both really liked, and were attracted to, each other. He asked you to come with him to Europe, but you were committed to college. You wrote each other romantic letters for about six months, at which point you started dating someone else, told him about it, and lost contact. Now, fifteen years later, he Googles you, finds your e-mail address, and suggests getting together when he comes to town on business. He writes he is now married with two young children but has never stopped thinking about your time together in college. He says you have greatly influenced his life, helping him to understand love and himself and that he has never loved anyone like that again.

Red Flags

- The relationship in the past was mostly long distance and he now once again wants to start a long-distance thing.
- Yes, you liked him back in college, but you don't really feel you knew him, or he you, or you yourself at that time, yet you had somehow profoundly influenced his life.
- He has been living one reality with his family but another in his mind.

ONLINE DATING

Like millions of men and women, you are trying to meet the right person online. You respond to a profile of a man who seems to have it all—good résumé, the right age, a great sense of humor, and a nice picture. The only problem: you gradually find out he wants to continue to e-mail, then IM, then talk on the phone for a rather long time. During a three-month period of almost daily communications, you both become increasingly open and intimate with each other. His "good night" calls are now a comforting part of your routine. When you suggest getting together, he can't, always having what seems to be a really good reason (working overtime this week, away this weekend, visiting his parents next weekend) and always reassuring you that he thinks this has great potential and that he can't wait to spend quality time together.

You would think this one is obvious, but as I've said before, when it comes to love our capacity for denial is unlimited. So here we go.

Red Flags

- Quantity matters. It's just going on for too long, demonstrating a commitment to the virtual rather than to using the virtual as a gate or pathway to the real. Don't ask me how much time is too long—I don't know. I just know that at some point *you'll* know it's too long.
- You are establishing an intimate connection and a dependency before you ever get to meet each other.
- The *details* make sense (e.g., he has good reasons as to why you can't meet), but the *whole* has no common sense (where there's a will, there's a way). So there's another,

unknown or unspoken reason he'd rather remain virtual. On your end, if you are looking for a relationship, why get attached to a virtual one? True, this is an emotional exchange, but it's more like reading a good novel than having a relationship with another person.

- One last thing: you don't know anything about this person—he could be a serial murderer . . .

In general, it might be useful to distinguish between meeting someone online (as in Match.com or similar dating services) and dating online. In the former situation, the Internet serves as a means to meeting and developing a relationship. In the latter, it serves to define the dynamic of the relationship, with the pattern of Virtual Love as the likely outcome.

EASY COME, EASY GO

You are a well-off, divorced, forty-eight-year-old woman who is looking to remarry. You meet a man through your college alumni organization. You live in New Jersey, he in Washington, but that's not a problem because you are mobile and willing to move given the right circumstances. After a couple of dates you fall madly in love and so does he. On your third date he starts talking about moving—maybe he would, maybe you would. Your only child is in college and he has two teenage children from a previous marriage, which is not a problem because you love him so much, you wouldn't mind being their stepmom. For the next couple of months you talk every day and you travel to see each other every weekend. You then go for a weeklong romantic vacation in Mexico, and after that you invite him to meet your friends. He says he is not ready. You are perplexed. You feel so comfortable with him, you push it. He says, No, I'm not ready to be part of your community.

This is a tough one, because your feelings were totally reciprocated, which makes the magic of love seem real. Nonetheless, there are reasons to be concerned . . .

Red Flags

- Such major life decisions as moving or becoming a stepparent are made, or at least proclaimed, on the basis of instant romantic love.
- Big problems (geography, children) are no problem, but small problems (meeting your friends) are insurmountable.
- The romance is wonderful, but it's all too quick, too much, and too easy.

WHERE THERE'S SMOKE, THERE'S FIRE

You sift through the e-mails that you received in response to the profile you posted on an online dating service. Almost all seem dull and inarticulate. If not, they are accompanied by an unattractive photo. Only one intrigues you: curious, funny, and skeptical, it makes you think there is actually a person there. You write back and exchange several e-mails. You learn that this man is a single architect, living with his parents in a suburb a mere half hour away. You ask him why he lives with his parents and about his past relationships. You get funny responses but no real answers. He does tell you that he suffers from "organ inferiority," and he then writes you a long e-mail about various amusing experiences and adventures he has had overseas. Then he doesn't respond to a couple of your e-mails. Then he writes another long e-mail, this time telling you about his college girlfriend and how she committed suicide while they were together. He then asks if you want to meet him for dinner, or maybe lunch or breakfast.

Red Flags

- At the risk of sounding like a cautious, conservative, boring know-it-all, who advocates a no-fun, risk-free life above all, this person's responses indicates he is not merely out of the box but, if you will, out of the cube: evasiveness, fragmented intimacy, and inconsistency are not exactly relationship building blocks.
- True, his responses could be a function of the medium—e-mails are tone deaf, and without the music the lyrics may well be misleading—which is to say, in person, his weirdness may not be so weird after all. Nevertheless, his string of decidedly off-beat informational tidbits raises real questions about his viability as a relationship candidate. When it comes to relationships, nine times out of ten, where there's smoke, there's fire.

HISTORY: HIS AND YOURS

You are a thirty-one-year-old single woman who never quite had a serious relationship. You tend to feel anxious around men you like and critical and withdrawn around those who like you. You meet someone online who lives about an hour and a half away, and after a couple of e-mails he comes to your town to get together for a Sunday brunch and an afternoon in the park. He is attractive in a boyish sort of way. He is smart, sensitive, and sincere. And he is a complete gentleman. As the date comes to an end, he tells you he really likes you and that he would like to get together again. You tell him you feel the same way. In truth, you can hardly believe how wonderful you feel. You're wondering if you finally met your soul mate, and you're thinking, "I'm falling in love." He then opens up more and tells you that while he is really looking for a relationship, he is hesitant because in previous relationships he always ended up losing interest, no matter how much he liked the girlfriend and how long he had tried to work it out.

Red Flags

- Your history: It's not a coincidence that you didn't have any serious relationships by age thirty-one. Something is holding you back and so it's unlikely that meeting your soul mate would be so simple.
- His history: the problem with his history is self-evident as he himself tells you—it's generally a good idea to listen to what people say and take it at face value.
- I can hear you say, "Okay, so I have a block and he has some baggage, so it won't be easy or simple, but people grow and change, so why assume we won't be able to work it out?" Fair enough, so you can try. The problem is, the long-distance aspect of the relationship may well be the reason you can fall in love so easily—you unconsciously know you won't have to deal with him in any kind of ongoing basis. And on his part, he may not lose interest in you for a long time for the same reason. So while it will look like your relationship is defying your history (and his), it will actually only reinforce it, and you will only realize this a year or two later when attempting to import the relationship from the virtual world to the real world.

Because of the repetition compulsion, we can never "overcome" or defy our history. But we can stop repeating it if, and only if, we are willing to learn from it. In this sense, the refrain "Those who are unwilling to remember the past are doomed to repeat it" is true not only in the life of nations but also of individuals. In our context, since the seven patterns of failed love are interrelated, you have to be aware not only of your Virtual Love history but of all your relationship patterns.

The scenarios above are all about Step One, Recognizing Your Pattern, in which we realize we are once again tempted by repetition. Many of us stay in unhealthy relationships, rationalizing that something is better than nothing and that we remain open to meeting new people. The problem is that if we continue to engage in old patterns we are not merely passing time. We actually reinforce these patterns, behaviorally, emotionally, and even biochemically—by strengthening the existing brain cell connections that guide these patterns along. But while deep down we know "it's not good for us," it's hard to give up on it, in part because truly embracing Step One might mean we may not have any relationship for some time or may have to explore relationships that initially feel all wrong.

This is precisely why we need Step Two, Understanding Your Ambivalence. Before we can move on to the uncharted territory of new love behaviors, we must know more about our emotional needs. We saw earlier how my patient Julie—after implementing Step One and eliminating virtual relationships from her life—was able to figure out what was most important for her in a man. As you may recall, the patient was able to do this when she became aware of her ambivalence about the type of man she wanted to be with and by reflecting about her family of origin, most particularly her relationship with her father. This is the general idea, and it can be done outside of therapy as well. So if, for example, you have ended a couple of virtual relationships and have resolved to avoid them in the future, don't stop there. Think about all your past relationships, including your family, boyfriends, close friends, and acquaintances.

Now what are some of the basic sensibilities or characteristics that appealed to you in these people? Was it intelligence or kindness? Creativity or sincerity? Ambition or good looks? Adventurousness or introspection? Assertiveness or patience? Empathy or sense of humor? You can also put it in the negative, listing those characteristics that hurt or bothered you the most (e.g., having a temper vs. being a doormat, being unpredictable vs. boring, needy vs. aloof).

In reality these attributes do not have to be an either-or proposition, but I put them in those terms in order to force you to choose between two equally appealing (or unappealing) characteristics so that your true bottom-line preference may emerge. This is a technique used in some psychological tests to overcome what social psychologists call the social desirability effect—our tendency to lie on personality tests in a manner that will make us look good. Since both responses are equally desirable in the abstract, forcing yourself to really think and make a choice will tell us something about who you really are. Of course, choosing in the abstract may not always correspond to reality. For example, you might *think* you need someone intellectually challenging, but in fact you might eventually find out that being emotionally supported is far more important to you. This is why you should draw this list of attributes from real people who have been significant in your life.

In addition to helping you know more about your bottom line, this forced-choice exercise will also prepare you for the fact that many important personal attributes *do* come in somewhat dichotomous, if not polar-opposite, forms. If you want someone who has both a great mind and a great body you are less likely to find him not only because all great things, particularly in combination, are statistical extremes, but also because, to some extent, in their development, great minds have become so because they needed to escape the physical, and great bodies have become so because they needed to avoid the brainy. By the same token, assertive, ambitious men are less likely to be supportive and sensitive, and sexy blondes—to partly confirm a rude stereotype—are less likely to be math professors.

So nobody's perfect, and you've got to get to know what you really want. But if Virtual Love has been one of your primary love patterns, in Step Two you need to consider your ambivalence not only about the imperfection of your love objects but also about love itself. In other words, in all likelihood, you have chosen Virtual Love not only to avoid dealing with the imperfections of those you might love but also to avoid too much closeness or intimacy. Ask yourself how much space and distance within a relationship you in fact might need—or can tolerate. If you are the type of person who likes to spend time on your own—reading, traveling alone, being casually social with occasional strangers—you might do well in a "parallel" relationship where you or your partner travel for business or reside in more than one place. If, on the other hand, you are someone who needs ongoing, daily closeness and values joint decision making, you might be better off in a "communal" relationship where you can hardly find time for yourself.

While the ideal may lie somewhere in the middle, in between these two models, those of us who repeatedly fall for Virtual Love may not be able to find it. A long-distance relationship reinforces either the enjoyment of separateness or the longing for togetherness and thus prevents you from knowing where you really fall on the continuum. So in Step Two, try to resolve in your own mind how much intimacy you really want. Now that you are no longer involved in virtual relationships, you are in a better position to know. Of course, if you have no relationship at all, you may feel lonely, which will influence your assessment. But here too you can use other kinds of relationships to get to your bottom line. What are your friendships, sibling relations, and relationships with your parents like? Do you talk to them and are you involved in their daily lives on a regular basis or only once in a while?

Engaging in the self-reflective work of Step Two—a process that, depending on individual circumstances, might take anywhere from a few days to a few years—will result in a degree of self-knowledge sufficient for undertaking Step Three. Now since Step Three involves accepting your ambivalence and your partner's "limitations," going through it actually requires being in a relationship. As we saw, my patient Julie implemented this step by adopting the logic of the Demosthenes Principle. She first tried to "improve" her partner so that she wouldn't be bothered by his limitations, but that backfired, making him seem even more limited. So she then found a way to embrace his limitations—not via a charitable attitude, as a good-hearted social worker or psychologist might do, but rather in her own selfish way, by making it work for her.

THE POSITIVE FLIP SIDE

As we saw in the previous chapter, "getting a life" and therefore not overfocusing on your partner's is a sure way of reducing ambivalence. If you must focus on your partner, however, at least be thorough. Don't be like the manager who, in reviewing his employee's work performance, checks in the strengths column "detail-oriented" and in the weaknesses column "loses the forest for the trees"—not realizing that people come in package deals and that his employee wouldn't have been on top of the details if he had not also been the type to lose the forest for the trees.

So if you must "review" your partner, make a list of the negative attributes that bother you and then list the positive flip side of these attributes. For example, if it upsets you—as it does many women—that your partner is unemotional and uncommunicative, think about the fact that he is logical and composed. Perhaps unlike your father or yourself, he doesn't have a temper, which is probably what drew you to him in the first place. You could probably get quite emotional—hurt or angry—and he wouldn't freak out on you. He could also be calm and reassuring when you are anxious about your health or about a problem with a family member or at work. All this is the positive flip side of his emotional numbness.

While refocusing on his positive flip sides will help you to accept your partner for who he is, it may be detrimental to the relationship in another way. If by way of accepting each other you globally label your partner as, say, "unfeeling" and yourself as "emotional," you define your differences as polar opposites, which means you will end up having little in common and a lot of conflict. In a self-fulfilling manner, you might become the one who wants to have intimate talks and he the one who wants to read the financial pages. Or you may become the one who always wants to go out, party, and spend money and he the one who likes to stay home, watch TV, and make a budget. Or you may become obsessed with shopping and he with philosophy. You get the picture.

To avoid this kind of polarization you shouldn't, as conventional wisdom would have it, simply compromise (as in "Okay, I'll see that stupid action movie this time if you see a romantic comedy with me next time"). Rather, you should work on integrating these polarities inside of you. In practical terms this means you should not only recognize and remember the positive flip sides in your partners but also engage with them. For example, if your "unemotional" or "uncommunicative" boyfriend mentions a setback or a problem at work, rather than asking him "How do you feel about it?" and having him answer it telegraphically, dismissively, or minimally and certainly without feelings, try to take a page from *his* book. Approach the situation as a problem to be fixed: ask him about his strategy for dealing with it, his long-term goal, his short-term tactics, his options for action, and the resources available to him.

If you engage your boyfriend in this kind of logical, rational manner, chances are that he will get more in touch with his feelings. This is because you wouldn't be scaring him with your feelings. The reason he is generally so calm and composed in the first place is that for some reason he is afraid of emotions—perhaps he had an overly emotional, smothering mother or maybe he associates emotion with weakness. So the more emotional you are, the more you push him to the "thinking, not feeling" corner. If, on the other hand, you work on doing more of the thinking and less of the feeling yourself, his emotions will emerge on their own—because they are there.

The purpose of this technique—engaging with the positive flip sides of your partner—is not to manipulate or induce a change in him. That's simply a likely by-product. The purpose is to stimulate a change within yourself—to take his positive flip side and try to learn from it, to emulate it and make it your own. This will make you a more balanced person and will eventually facilitate a parallel change in your partner. If you stop spending too much money, he will stop budgeting all the time; if you start enjoying staying home more, he will start wanting to go out more; if you develop an interest in politics he will become interested in your relationship with your sister . . .

To summarize, in Step Three you identify the positive flip side of the negative attribute you don't like in your partner. This helps you to accept your partner for who he is and also to learn from him by adopting his positive flip side yourself, which ultimately leads to a lessening in his negative attribute. So paradoxically, by accepting his limitations you end up helping him to outgrow them, which further reduces your ambivalence. I will return to this technique—with more practical suggestions of how to use it—when discussing Step Three in chapter 3.

VIRTUAL LOVE IN LONG-TERM RELATIONSHIPS

In long-term relationships or marriages, we are more likely to be aware of our ambivalence. For one thing, being able to tolerate ambivalence is a prerequisite for remaining committed to a relationship. This is why you often hear married people teasing each other about their various ridiculous, rigid, or irritating personality traits. Sometimes it's just good-natured teasing, but often enough it reflects the bitterness and unhappiness of living with unresolved ambivalence. Being stuck in that phase is a common form of unhappiness that gives marriage some of its bad reputation. In this kind of marriage or relationship, using the positive flip-side technique consistently and diligently can make a huge difference.

Let's consider a not atypical, forty-something New York couple with a significant Virtual Love aspect in their marriage. He is a successful investment banker with a job requiring 25 percent to 50 percent travel. She is a housewife and a mother. He is into his career and she is into the children, running the household, playing tennis, and volunteering. He also likes golfing and skiing, which he does whenever possible on business trips but also when he's home, with friends, on the weekend. This lifestyle has evolved gradually over the years, and the couple has always thought of it as temporary. "I'm not going to be able to work like this forever," the husband would say, adding, "I'll make enough money for us to live comfortably and then I'll retire or find something more low-key." The wife would accept this, thinking, "Another year or two of this won't kill me." But as a year turns into five, and five into ten, this form of acceptance develops into frustration, anger, and eventually bitter resignation. Over the years, one would repeatedly hear the wife complaining to family and friends, "He's never home," "At least he should be here on the weekends," "He missed our son's recital again," or "He doesn't spend any time with the children." And the husband would gripe to his friends or coworkers that his wife is always on his case, that he can't get out on the weekends, that he has to call her twelve times a day when away, and so on and so forth.

But if at this point, the wife accepts that this lifestyle is not a coincidence but rather something she chose and continues to choose every day, she can start identifying the positive flip side of her husband's escape from intimacy. He is independent, he doesn't interfere with her running of the house, and he doesn't expect her to be there for him with dinner on the table every night. Having been the one left behind, needy, lonely, and critical of his absence up to this point, she can now learn something from him. She can start being more independent—perhaps go back to school, develop new, more intense friendships outside of the marriage, or maybe even travel to Asia on her own. If she follows that path she would end up needing less of her husband's time and energy and less intimacy from their relationship. This, in turn, would make the husband miss her more and want more intimacy with her, which sooner or later would lead him to make adjustments in his work schedule or lifestyle.

The outcome of this realignment in the couple's dynamic will be one of a "parallel" marriage in which both husband and wife accept—perhaps even embrace—the level of Virtual Love which exists in their relationship. For these individuals, limiting the degree of intimacy in the relationship may be ideal. One complication, which you may want to consider if you plan to have a family, is that this lifestyle is not ideal for children. Another question is whether this type of relationship can survive the kind of change brought about by a loss of job, declining health, or retirement. Will this couple make it if forced by circumstance to be together on a daily basis? There is no way to predict, of course, but my experience with patients suggests that much depends on the extent to which the couple's lifestyle reflects a deep psychological structure in one or both of the individuals. For example, if you are a successful concert pianist with a career involving constant traveling, chances are you were able to dedicate yourself to this career in the first place *because,* psychologically speaking, you didn't need or couldn't deal with the daily goings-on of intimacy. In this case, an external change in lifestyle requiring that you spend most of your time at home with your partner would indeed put the relationship at risk.

By comparison, if you are a midlevel manager in a large company, who after five years on the job is offered a once-in-a-lifetime promotion opportunity requiring 50 percent travel, and you are torn because you don't want to be away from your family yet after a lot of agonizing you end up taking the job, you are probably in a different category. Even if this new opportunity keeps you traveling for the next ten years, and your marriage becomes more and more virtual, a job change requiring you to be back home all the time is not likely to be as threatening to you. This is so because your work choice was driven less by a deep, characterological need for interpersonal space and more by external circumstances.

In reality, of course, things are not so clear-cut. For example, one patient, an actor, ended up with a dual residence, one in New York where he would perform on Broadway and one in Los Angeles where he would do TV. Was he drawn to a career involving bicoastal commuting or to one involving performing, in which travel was a necessary evil? After working on this for a while we came to see it was both. Nonetheless, there was an early indication of his strong need for interpersonal space when I asked him in our first session how often he saw his boyfriend of a year and a half. "I actually saw him only twice in the past year," he said casually, betraying neither cognitive dissonance nor palpable unhappiness over the situation.

Now while the conflict between our needs for intimacy and for solitude is as ancient as love itself, it seems that modern life has made it more possible than ever before to have long-term, long-distance relationships. One of my favorite examples is the story of a patient whose life demonstrated, among other things, that it's never too late to change the patterns of failed love. The patient, Elisabeth, came to see me at the age of fifty-two in the midst of a serious depression, which in her case was brought about not by a biological condition, not even so much by the betrayal and loss she had suffered, but rather by the death of an illusion.

Elisabeth grew up in small, rural town in northern Wisconsin. Her parents owned a small grocery store and the family, which included Elisabeth, her two older sisters, and her maternal grandmother, lived in a small two-bedroom apartment upstairs. All this, and the family's poor sense of boundaries—sex was discussed and engaged in for the children to hear and see and the mother discussed her daughters loudly with customers in the store, to cite just a couple of examples—made Elisabeth, the girl, fantasize about getting away. As a teenager she daydreamed about traveling, and finally, in college, she decided to become a flight attendant. Being pretty, smart, and adventurous, this was not too hard for Elisabeth to accomplish. A couple of years later she became a full-time flight attendant with a major airline, working the New York–Paris route.

It was thus at the workplace—on an airplane—that she met Jean-Paul, the man who would become her husband. An international French banker returning home from a business trip, he struck up a flirtatious conversation with her. "One thing led to another," and they started dating on the weekends, her time off. After several months Elisabeth found out that Jean-Paul was married. However, he was unhappy in his marriage and in love with Elisabeth so shortly thereafter he divorced his wife and married Elisabeth.

For a while they "lived" in Paris—still on the weekends, her time off. When they decided to have children, Elisabeth wanted the kids to grow up American so they decided to relocate to New York. Now it was his turn to commute, which he did for the next twenty years, as they raised two children and continued to have an active but stable lifestyle. They both loved skiing, traveling, and socializing, and at some point, when Elisabeth felt the children needed a full-time mother, she left her job and stayed with them in New York, enjoying the challenges of parenthood. Since Jean-Paul's high-paying job required that he stay in Paris, and because Elisabeth didn't want to move her children to Europe, they decided to continue their parallel lifestyle.

Clearly, for Elisabeth, the desire to get away from her family had influenced her professional choice. But it also colored her choice of a husband. She chose someone who was involved with another woman and who lived in a different country. In other words, to counteract her childhood experience of interpersonal suffocation, she chose to protect herself from too much intimacy. While she never quite verbalized it that way, Elisabeth knew that this lifestyle worked for her, and she was generally happy. A couple of times over the years she was disturbed when her husband wasn't where he was supposed to be and couldn't be reached by phone and when a friend told her she had seen him with another woman. But not wanting to get into a fight, she accepted Jean-Paul's explanations and moved on.

Nonetheless, all this came to a crashing halt—some twenty-five years into the marriage—when Elisabeth, on a visit to their Paris house, found a letter written to Jean-Paul by another woman, Simone, discussing their . . . living arrangement! It turned out that for the past nineteen years Jean-Paul had had another life. He had another house in a suburb of Paris, where he "lived" with another woman from Monday to Friday. Over the years he would also go on short "business" trips (i.e., vacations) with this woman.

When confronted with this discovery, Jean-Paul didn't deny it. He explained his perspective and told Elisabeth he would be happy to continue the existing arrangement but that if she wanted a divorce, he would be financially generous.

This was when Elisabeth came to see me. She felt betrayed, rejected, and humiliated, but more than anything else she was devastated by the discovery that her husband was not the person she thought he was. Sure, she knew he was independent and she could even understand if he'd had some "casual thing" on a business trip. But for him to engage in a deception of this magnitude—a double life—could only mean that she really didn't know who he was and that their relationship had been an illusion. Of course, in retrospect, the signs were there, as they always are, but Elisabeth chose to ignore them *in order to avoid facing the truth about her husband.* The truth was that in addition to being a generous, fun-loving, and kind man, he was also a dishonest, manipulative, and hostile man.

So while for many years their lifestyle supported Elisabeth's illusion about who her husband was, she now plunged into a crisis of ambivalence. "Should I stay in the marriage or should I go?" she asked me in the first session. For the first time in twenty-five years, Elisabeth was aware of her ambivalence about her husband and their relationship. In terms of our three steps, we can say it took Elisabeth all these years to get to Step One.

Naturally, I didn't answer Elisabeth's question, and it took her almost a year to reach a decision. For one thing, Elisabeth knew that she was well suited to the parallel lifestyle she had chosen and that she couldn't deal with a needy, demanding man. But as we delved into her history, we found out that much of her desire to get away from her family was defensive and secondary in nature. Like every child, she *did* want the intimacy of being known and accepted by her parents. But since in her family, intimacy was exercised in an overbearing, smothering manner, she embraced the other extreme. Yet underneath—precisely because her emotional needs had not been met at a young age—she was more needy than most. Realizing this in therapy, Elisabeth was finally able to reach Step Two, and she decided to end her virtual marriage and to look for relationships with real intimacy.

For the next five years I continued to see Elisabeth in therapy, but notwithstanding all this work she was unable to meet a man to her liking. She had plenty of dates all right, but almost without exception, she was left uninspired. Indeed, compared with her previous lifestyle, dating and getting to know "the local boys," as she would put it, was a rather dreary proposition. However, Elisabeth remained relentless about her bottom line: no more Jean-Pauls. And she also made progress in therapy, learning how to be more intimate and real—at least with her therapist. At this point she decided to terminate the therapy to try to implement what she had learned, on her own.

It is not unusual for patients to leave treatment before the therapist think they should, or before he knows "the end" of their story. I therefore often welcome hearing from such patients later on. But I was particularly happy to hear from Elisabeth—because of the nature of her news. Her letter came several years later, about ten years after she separated from Jean-Paul. It turned out that after terminating her treatment she moved to be near her daughter who was raising a family in a small Minnesota town. There, Elisabeth met, fell in love with, and married a divorced man who was also in his early sixties, and whom she felt was her true soul mate. The interesting thing was that this man—while also a foreigner, originally from Sweden—was quite the opposite of Jean-Paul. A retired farmer and a "homebody," who was very involved with his adult children, he was interested in spending as much time as possible with Elisabeth and in working on their new house together.

So Elisabeth came full circle. Having first escaped her family and intimacy to the world of international jet-setting and a virtual marriage, she ended up in the Midwest, in a lifestyle more similar to that of her childhood. In doing so, she achieved Step Three on her own. She now accepted a part of herself—her dependency needs—which she had previously denied. She was therefore able to accept and to love someone with similar needs. At the same time, she didn't regret her previous relationship, knowing full well that it too represented a part of herself. And she also knew that when the initial idealization of her new husband wore off, she would have ambivalent feelings, wishing at times that he could be more like Jean-Paul.

3

One-Way Love

He placed his hand
Where he had hoped and felt the heart still beating
Under the Bark
OVID

CUPID'S SPLIT

In a typical act of revenge and mischief, Cupid, the infamous boy-god of love, struck Apollo with an arrow, causing him to fall in love, and Daphne with an arrow, driving her away from love. So naturally, when Apollo, the god of music and poetry, approached Daphne, the beautiful nymph started to run away from him. Chasing Daphne, Apollo begged, cajoled, and promised her the world. But Daphne only responded by running faster. After a long chase, realizing she was about to be captured, the nymph prayed that the body that so attracted Apollo would be changed and destroyed forever. And her wish was granted: her limbs grew numb and heavy, her arms turned into branches, her hair became leaves, and her breasts were "closed" with delicate bark. At that moment, as Daphne transformed into a laurel tree, Apollo caught up with her. He longingly embraced her, still loving her, and feeling her fading heartbeat under the bark.

The pain of One-Way Love touches anyone who's ever been disappointed in love. In fact, because the pain of love is so much a part of even so-called healthy love, we instinctively tend to identify with love's underdog and to have more sympathy for the rejected than the rejecter. This kind of identification is one of the reasons that *The Sorrows of Young Werther*—Goethe's nineteenth-century novel about a young man who kills himself because of One-Way Love—touched off a series of suicides all over Europe.

But identifying and empathizing with the pain of One-Way Love—which is the term I use for the inclination to fall in love or to be drawn to emotionally unavailable people—is only one aspect of our reaction to it. We also wonder why it is that someone who repeatedly falls in love with unavailable people is also repeatedly unavailable to those who are interested in him. I can hardly count the number of patients who, over the years, have bemoaned their apparent fate to be attracted to people who wouldn't reciprocate their feelings while at the same time themselves being unable to reciprocate the feelings of those attracted to them. This is the universal experience of Cupid's Split, where we try to cope with our ambivalence toward love by dividing the world of love objects into attractive and unattractive extremes. By doing so we can hold on to the fantasy of perfect beauty, intelligence, and spirituality and thereby cling to the illusion of pure love.

But as universal as Cupid's Split is, the degree of the fissure it creates in our relationships depends on our individual history and character. For example, a patient's father abandoned the family when she was a young child, and her stepfather—the mother remarried a couple of years later—forcefully insisted that she immediately accept him as her father. In adulthood, this woman would fall deeply in love with unavailable men—an engaged man, a gay man, and others who were simply not interested in her—while always warding off other men who were, as she put it, "imposing" themselves on her.

Although this illustrates how one's particular life story—in this case, the patient's unconscious desire to attain the longed-for father and to discard the unwanted one—can contribute to the formation of a repetitive love pattern, this patient was hardly the first or last woman to divide men into the "perfect though unavailable" versus the "available but not good enough" categories. At the same time, the majority of men (and women) are neither perfect nor completely unacceptable (to someone). Those of us prone to One-Way Love create this split in our mind in order to support the illusion that love itself can be perfect. While some people, like the patient above, would have to address in therapy the original family trauma, others could deal more directly with their One-Way Love pattern—in or out of therapy.

STEP ONE: RECOGNIZING YOUR PATTERN

Because the person we are drawn to in this pattern is physically available—sometimes he is actually dating you—it can be difficult to identify the pattern early on. If, like many of my patients, you are in a long-term relationship with a man who won't commit, it's easy to view *him* as the problem, rationalizing that *he* is not ready yet or *he* is the "commitment phobe." And if you are serially attracted to unavailable men or women, it's tempting to see yourself as the unlucky victim of coincidence; or if you don't believe in luck and you live in a big city, to blame it on statistics—more single women than men; or if you are more psychologically minded, to feel "there's something wrong with me."

It would be more useful, however, in these situations, to examine the way in which *you*, rather than your love object, is unavailable. This is because the amount of psychic energy you invest in unavailable people is equal to the amount of psychic energy you invest in avoiding available people. In other words, in Step One, Recognizing Your Pattern, you must understand and accept your own Cupid's Split. *It's Cupid, stupid!*

Patients in psychotherapy often resist this idea. To begin with, they don't even notice the advances or gestures of interest on the part of people they are not attracted to. Then, when they acknowledge that some people are at times interested in them, they insist that these people are "losers" or in some other way inferior to the unavailable ones. But my case for Cupid's Split is often clinched when we find that the patient applies his split to one and the same person. This was the case with a female lawyer who, using her training and natural inclination, managed to raise reasonable doubt even in my mind as to whether her history of pursuing unavailable men was a pattern. Just as I was getting ready to consider her detailed and logical explanation of how each of her relationships or situations had a unique set of circumstances, she "stumbled" and volunteered that her most significant relationship, which lasted about a year and a half, could offer some highly relevant evidence.

"It started with his pursuing me, and I was not really interested. We dated a few times, and even had sex, but basically I cooled it down and started dating someone else. But than he stopped calling and I called him a couple of times. He finally returned my call and we started dating again except that now the tables were turned. I was really into him and he didn't seem all that interested. At some point we decided to date exclusively, but after a while I realized he wasn't the right person for me so I ended it. At that time, of course, he once again started pursuing me . . ."

So first the patient wasn't interested because the other person *was,* and then she *was* because the other person *wasn't.* In other words, the patient's one longer-term relationship had both sides of Cupid's Split, which, sadly enough, was the main reason it lasted that long. A more extreme case was that of a woman who canceled her engagement to a man she had dated for two years because she felt smothered by him. She later moved from her California hometown to New York and at some point came to see me for therapy. After a year in therapy, in which she insisted she was not at all drawn to unavailable men, she heard from a mutual friend that her former fiancé—who in the meantime had gotten married—might be getting a divorce. My patient then let her former fiancé know, through the mutual friend, that she had rethought their relationship and would like him to contact her. Though she did not hear from him, she was convinced he would want her back, and partly on that basis she decided to move back to California. When we explored this before she left, the patient rationalized that when she had canceled their engagement years earlier, she was not ready to commit to a man who in fact offered her a real, intimate relationship. "But I'm ready now," she said. "And I just know he's still thinking of me." What she was un-willing to acknowledge, however, was that the passage of time, the magnitude of the geographical divide, and the fact that he didn't respond to her message all made it easy to forget the emo-tional impact of his smothering neediness. Upon leaving New York, the patient promised to let me know if anything happened with this man in LA. But I did not hear from her until a couple of years later when she got married . . . to another man.

And another variation on the theme: A thirty-year-old man came to see me after realizing he had made a "terrible mistake" a couple of years earlier in ending a ten-year relationship when his girlfriend gave him a marriage ultimatum. This relationship, he explained, had it all—compatibility, passion, communication.

It's just that he wasn't ready at the time. And ever since then he'd been dating women who didn't really turn him on or trying to date women who wouldn't reciprocate. But a more detailed questioning revealed that the old, ideal relationship sustained several low periods and a couple of separations, all triggered when he and the girlfriend literally took turns losing interest.

This kind of relationship makes it impossible to claim that it's something in the other person you are drawn to or repelled by. Of course, there is always something about the other person we react to, but in the case of One-Way Love the glue to the relationship is the glimmer of unavailability. In practical terms, this means that if in addition to being attracted to unavailable people you've also had a relationship of this kind, you can be fairly certain you are under the "curse" of Cupid's Split.

If you didn't have such a relationship, you can still diagnose your own Cupid's Split by applying certain (loosely) quantitative as well as qualitative analyses to your experiences. On the quantitative side: If you had several relationships or attempted relationships with unavailable people and you are in your late twenties, you should be concerned; make a list of the number of people who have been interested in you over the years, and get ready to accept that you are gripped by the pattern of One-Way Love. If you are in your thirties with this history, you should be more than concerned—perhaps skip to Step Two, Understanding Your Ambivalence, on p. 98; if you are in your early twenties, however, you needn't worry yet, unless your gut feeling tells you otherwise. A caveat: given that it sometimes takes a long time to correct the patterns of failed love, being aware in your early twenties—for women in particular, giving the looming biological clock of the thirties—may not be such a bad idea after all.

On the qualitative side: Notice if you call again when a prospective date doesn't return your call or if you call him when he says he'll call but doesn't; note if you obsessively discuss with friends the meaning of his failure to respond; note if you once again propose to get together when you run into him; and note if you don't take it at face value when he says relationships are not a priority for him. If you've done any of these things more than once or twice, chances are you're in trouble. Chances are you've also participated in creating the other side of Cupid's Split, though that may be more difficult to diagnose. Let me illustrate.

A single man in his thirties has been dating a woman for a couple of months. "I really like her," he says, "and I don't want to screw it up." He goes on to explain that he is worried he will soon lose interest and will start feeling obligated and burdened, which is what usually happens to him. "I hope it works out because this girl is not the needy type—she's independent and she doesn't mind that I have outside activities." But in the next session the patient relates the first fight of the relationship, which erupted because he failed to call when he said he would. He was out to dinner with an out-of-town male friend and told the girlfriend he would call when they finished eating so that she could join them for drinks. But instead, for no reason he could articulate, he didn't call until 11 p.m. As a result, the girlfriend waited for his call, was unable to make other plans for the evening, and was mad at him when she picked up the phone. So even though he said he liked the fact that she was not needy or dependent, in not calling on time he actually went about creating these emotional states in her. Predictably, her reaction made him feel obligated and burdened, which in turn made her feel needier and which, of course, resulted in his wanting to get out of the relationship. In short, contrary to his conscious intention, and without even realizing it, he had created his own unavailability.

Another patient, an extremely attractive and pleasant woman, reported that nothing was ever happening on her dates. When we examined the details of her dating behavior, it became clear that she was actually "working" on not letting anything happen. For example, one man started talking about a previous relationship on his second date with her. This made the patient conclude he "had baggage" and "needed" her to listen to him. Not wanting a relationship with someone needy, she didn't respond, which, of course, only created more neediness in him.

Similarly, when another man said on their third date that he was "afraid of affection," she thought, "He has issues," and ignored his statement, only making his "issue" more pressing for him and perhaps in her mind too. Finally, when a man she quite liked tried to hold her hand on their first date, she went along even though she didn't feel comfortable with it. In this last example, she thought she was "giving it a chance," but in fact, by colluding with something she didn't like, she was doing just the opposite, forming an obligation and a desire to get away and, ultimately, her own unavailability. Had she removed her hand or said "no," she would have found out if this man was in fact needy or just a little forward.

These are small, daily examples that in great accumulation put your relationship or dating experiences on the trajectory of One-Way Love. Analyzing and bringing to a halt such behaviors is one of the hallmarks of psychotherapy. But it can also be done outside of therapy and must be done if you want to change your pattern. To do it on your own, you must reflect on your relationships with the following mantra in mind: "what I feel/think/say I want is only half of the story; the other half is to be found in the interpersonal consequence of what I do." So if you think you want a relationship but you're pursuing someone who doesn't appear to respond, think again: since your action results in pushing him away further, it suggests you don't really want a relationship; you might want to want a relationship but you don't. And conversely, if you think you are "giving someone a chance" by kissing him even if you don't feel like it, think about how you'll feel after the kiss.

STEP TWO: UNDERSTANDING YOUR AMBIVALENCE

As we saw before, and will see again in subsequent chapters, in Step Two you need to figure out what you really want from a relationship and a partner—what's your bottom line. In addition, you have to accept the obvious—though you have previously worked so hard to deny it—which is that you will only have a relationship with one of those available types whom up to now you've rejected or even failed to notice. Actually, from this pool of candidates or type, we have to subtract those who, mirror image–like, were only interested in you because you were unavailable to them. So the number of the "undesirables" from whom you'll have to choose is actually smaller than what you might imagine. And to make this bleak picture truly depressing, the older you get—into your late thirties and forties—the smaller the supply of what you might think of as acceptable candidates. It is perhaps crude to speak of love as a function of market economy, but in reality, I'm afraid it is, in the sense that the best candidates are picked early. This means that starting at some point, the longer you wait the more imperfect the potential partners will be, and therefore, the more ambivalent you will feel in every dating situation. This ugly market condition is worse for women, since in our culture it is more acceptable and practicable for men to marry younger women, which further limits the supply of suitable men. If this analysis makes you anxious, use this anxiety to spring into action. If it makes you angry, perhaps you are still in denial.

But the good news is that these grim market conditions can serve to drive home the central fact about love: *It's all in our head anyway.* Although our capacity for love is located deep in the more primitive part of our brain and is therefore illogical, in subtle ways it can still be influenced by its interactions with the more advanced, cognitive part of our brain. Like other emotions, love cannot be willed; however, it can be invited to visit. By saying yes to love, we cognitively commit to creating the conditions for a new kind of relationship to emerge. It's not that we jump at the first available person coming our way, but rather, knowing we are going to feel ambivalent no matter what, we stop looking for reasons to flee and start looking for reasons to stay.

Saying yes to love is not that simple, I acknowledge, but there is a surprising degree of simple decision making to it. Consider the following examples. One of my patients always felt pressured to spend more time with his girlfriend than he wanted to. At some point he agreed to go on a weeklong cruise with her. When the time arrived he was apprehensive about spending so much time together and was worried that he would feel smothered. "I will not be surprised if I break up with her when we get back," he said before leaving on vacation. But in his first session back he sounded a completely different note: "We had a wonderful time together. Once I realized there was no escape, I relaxed, and after a couple of days I felt I could be with her forever."

Oh well, if it were only that simple, I'd recommend a cruise to all my ambivalent patients and . . . go out of business. Indeed, this patient did not end up committing to his girlfriend. Nonetheless, temporary as it may have been, the change in his attitude—particularly the counterintuitive nature of the change—was illuminating.

Another patient revealed to his pregnant wife that he had doubts about their marriage. Pointing to her stomach, the wife said, "Well, that's too bad because now you're trapped." Like the patient above, this one too reacted counterintuitively—with a sense of relief. Because she confirmed to him what he kind of knew anyway—that he wouldn't leave her now that she was pregnant—he was able to accept his ambivalence, at least for the time being. After all, what's the point of holding on to ambivalence if it's not "actionable"? A similar dynamic sometimes occurs with couples who get pregnant "accidentally," early in their relationship. If they have difficulty committing, they will use the pregnancy as an excuse to get married even before they are "fully ready." Of course, in some cases this can spell trouble for the future but not if the couple accepts the psychological principle underlying all these examples.

Whereas many of us think we'll only be able to commit when we meet "the right person" (i.e., someone about whom we are not ambivalent), the truth is that we can only resolve our ambivalence *after* we commit. This is so because as long as we think there is an out, we have no incentive to accept our ambivalence. If my boyfriend is too short, I'll look for a taller man next time; if he's too passive, I'll look for someone more assertive; if he's a little boring, I'll find someone more exciting; if he is too angry, I'll replace him with someone sweet; if he is not smart enough . . . well, you get the picture.

If, on the other hand, I believe that I am stuck with this imperfect person, I'll make it my business to accept his limitations. This principle can be applied more generally to many important life decisions. So while many people struggle with indecisiveness about important career path or job offer decisions because they think there is a right and a wrong decision to be made, I believe this is often false. If anything, a difficult decision-making situation may indicate that *there is no* right or wrong decision. It's therefore up to us not to make the right decision but to make the decision right—*after* we've made it.

This principle, in a sense, is the rationale for the notion of arranged marriages. While I'm not recommending this as a solution, it does seem that societies in which arranged marriages are the norm do just as well as ours, if not better, in the love department. This is beautifully portrayed in the movie *Monsoon Wedding*, in which an Indian girl is torn between her passionate affair with an unavailable (married) man and her family's plans for her wedding. Because she thinks she is in love with the married man, she keeps feeling she can't go on with the wedding plans. But when she finally lets go of the affair, she allows herself to "go with the flow" of her overwhelming family and culture. She meets the intended groom and proceeds to fall in love with him too.

It is noteworthy that in an arranged marriage the parents or matchmaker carefully pick the candidate they think is appropriate. Again, without buying into this notion, there is something to be learned from it. Before saying yes to love, you do want to know that the basic ingredients of compatibility are there. To me this means that whatever differences in personality there are, they should be subsumed by a similarity of philosophy, values, and sensibilities. In that sense, it's not all that different from a close friend. This type of similarity does not guarantee love, but it creates the conditions for love, if not to occur, then at least to succeed if it does occur. At the very least it protects you from falling in love with or committing to the wrong person. So in a way, we must refine the decision-making principle from above: it's not that there is no Mr. Right and Mr. Wrong; it's just that there is more than one Mr. Right and no Mr. Perfect (and yes, there is a Mr. Wrong, in fact many of them).

In another twist to this principle—actually a complete reversal but one that nevertheless provides further evidence that it's "all in your head"—we can also say yes to love by "pretending" that we are *not* committing. Rather than trap yourself and then feel you must resolve your ambivalence, you can commit to your partner in action but continue to feel that there is always an out, so that you don't have to leave *today*. This may sound flip, but bear with me—there's a serious philosophical and psychological concept at play here, and some of my patients have used it quite successfully.

One patient came to see me after he was devastated by the breakup of a relationship with a woman who was never fully available. He met her on an airplane, pursued her long distance, and eventually moved halfway across the country to be with her. But she remained noncommittal even while living together, until finally breaking up with him and breaking his heart. Sometime later the patient got into a relationship in which he was the unavailable party and that he ended after two years. This last relationship was more typical for him: getting involved with a woman but with time feeling suffocated and wanting out.

After exploring his pattern of One-Way Love and seeing that his Cupid's Split was a historical repetition of his relationship with his mother—he was intensely attached to her in his early years but later basically wrote her off—the patient decided he was fed up with his pattern. He was therefore finally able to fall in love with an available woman and also to recognize that sooner or later he would begin to feel smothered and want to withdraw. He therefore told his girlfriend, and himself, "I'd like to continue to see each other and do all the things we do, but let's just not call it a relationship." So they continued to see each other and eventually moved in together without ever referring to their "relationship." They never talked about whether they should move in together or what that would mean in terms of their commitment. They just did it. They then stopped using birth control and she got pregnant. Again, they didn't really talk about it, though they knew exactly what it meant. Then they got married in a small wedding, without much fanfare, again, not really for themselves, but for their families.

This might seem silly and may raise an objection as to how can it ever be good for a couple not to talk about such matters. But for this patient it was an effective and successful way to deal with his ambivalence. Since the patient "voted with his feet," the girlfriend didn't have a reason to question his commitment. And by not labeling his gradually increased level of commitment, the patient was able to preserve the notion that he was only committing one day at a time and that he could always exit tomorrow. This, of course, is the truth about our commitments, as is painfully evident by the prevalence of divorce. So silly, profound, or both, "pretending" that our commitment is temporary can work.

The above case must be distinguished from the all-too-common situation in which enjoying but not talking about the relationship is a sign that one of the partners, more typically the man, is available now, but is not willing to commit, and the other, more typically the woman, colludes with the silence out of not wanting to hear the truth. Perhaps like my patient, in this kind of a relationship, the man is also trying to manage his ambivalence. But unlike my patient, he does so without conscious awareness. His game is to try to have it both ways by not making a choice.

Now since both types of men do not talk, the question for their potential partners is how to know which is which. The general principle is, watch what your man *does*, not what he says or doesn't say. This, I believe, is particularly useful when dealing with men, most of whom still subscribe to the unconscious philosophy that talk is cheap and that actions speak louder than words.

A more universal example of "pretending" was evident in a patient, who, once recognizing her One-Way Love pattern, got engaged and married a few months into a new relationship. The patient had a good marriage for several years, but then she and her husband started to fight. Their fights, which were about what each of them wasn't getting from the relationship, escalated and increased in frequency for a good couple of years. Finally, they both felt they couldn't take it anymore and they decided to separate. But as soon as they made the decision, they let go of their anger, and they started having a good time together, relaxing and laughing in a manner delightfully reminiscent of the early phases of their relationship. At this point, all the arguments about his needs and her needs seemed to lose their relevance—it was as if they never took place. So the patient and her husband just stayed together.

This is a bit of an exaggeration, because while they didn't discuss those fights at the time, each in his or her own way quietly worked to accommodate the needs of the other person. But the point is, once they "pretended" they were separating—reminding themselves, so to speak, that they were free to go—they were able to stay. This, indeed, is one of the productive functions of "stupid" fights so common even in the best of relationships—to reestablish a sense of separateness and independence so that we can continue to stay together.

So in saying yes to love, we can commit, by pretending that we are trapped or by pretending that we are free. Strangely, in either strategy, what we are "pretending" is true: we are committed *and* we are free. But when our ambivalence tortures us, we seem to forget—that's when we truly pretend—one or the other. So if you are tormented by the allure of a better Mr. Right, you need to remember you are committed and forget you are free; if you are tormented by the fear of being imprisoned, you need to remember you are free and forget you are committed.

Much like in the pattern of Virtual Love, your Cupid's Split indicates that you have a conflict about intimacy. This is important to be aware of, even after you commit to a relationship. For one thing, you should claim your right for solitude, space, and separateness *up front* so that you don't end up acting out later. And you should also give that space to your partner. In my experience, many married men who develop secret lives away from home do so, in part, because they feel controlled by, or not sufficiently separated from, their spouses. It is also the case, however, that too much separation can bring about the same outcome.

In many relationships, one partner is chronically needy, feeling that the other is more interested in his work, in playing golf, in his friends, or in spending time alone, while the other partner struggles with wanting to get away and feeling guilty and obligated. This dynamic is self-perpetuating as long as you expect your partner to change. Telling your partner "You should spend less time with your friends and more with me" only results in his feeling more obligated and guilty and therefore further wanting to get away from you. Likewise, telling your partner "You need to be more independent and do more of your own thing" only reinforces her feelings that you don't want to be with her and therefore her need for more. If, on the other hand, you are aware of your own conflict regarding intimacy—your own need for togetherness as well as separateness—you can simply change yourself, which will also change the relationship.

If you are the "needy" partner, get a life and do your own thing—this will help him to get in touch with his need for you. And if you are the "independent" partner, stop living out of obligation and start spending time with your partner when you actually *want* to and doing things with her that you *want* to do, all of which will make her feel more loved and less needy. This kind of integration and its impact on the relationship brings us into the territory of Step Three.

STEP THREE: RESOLVING YOUR AMBIVALENCE

As we saw in the previous chapter, resolving your ambivalence involves (1) identifying the positive flip side of the attribute you don't like in your partner, (2) accepting him for who he is, and (3) taking on his positive flip side yourself, a by-product of which is the eventual decrease in his negative attribute (see pages 79–82). The same Step Three applies here, and to help you use it in your relationships I've created a table of Flip-Side Conversions (see below). From left to right, the table lists common negative attributes, the flip side of each, and the advantage it holds for you. Reviewing the entire table first will help you to get perspective on the kinds of things that bug you in your partner, potential or actual. Then find the negative attribute(s) that may bother you in your partner, and identify its positive flip side and what's in it for you. Remember this, and remind yourself of it every time you are bothered by one of your partner's personality traits.

FLIP-SIDE CONVERSIONS

Negative Attribute	Positive Flip Side	What's in It for You
1. Doesn't express emotions	Logical and calm	He doesn't have a temper. He thinks clearly about problems. You can express *your* emotions.
2. A bad planner, irresponsible about scheduling and details, loses and forget things	Spontaneous, flexible, fun-loving	You are in control of the schedule. Life is not boring. He surprises you with gifts or ideas.

Negative Attribute	Positive Flip Side	What's in It for You
3. A neatness freak, rigid, obsessive	Organized and disciplined, on top of details, thoughtful	He does the dusting. You don't have to worry about boring details.
4. A bad dresser	Doesn't put on airs	You can relax about *your* appearance You can be yourself.
5. A bit boring	Reliable	He'll always be there. He'll always find *you* interesting.
6. Introverted, quiet, not outgoing	A good listener, considerate, patient	You get heard. You get to be the life of the party. You get to choose friends and events.
7. Critical, demanding, angry, has temper	Self-critical, involved, expresses his emotions, not apathetic/depressed	You can criticize *him*, express *your* frustrations, get angry directly and openly.
8. Restless, needs constant stimulation, wants to discuss politics/ business/philosophy/ all the time	Knowledgeable, interesting, entertaining	He gets you to do things. You get an education.
9. Watches CNN/ football/golf all the time	Not in your face	You can talk on the phone, read, visit your mother.
10. Doesn't make enough money	Spends more time at home	You have more intimacy, more equality.
11. A workaholic	Gets things done, good provider	You have time, independence, more money.
12. Physically not in shape	A thinking person	You don't have to be in perfect shape, you get to feel attractive and strong, you can talk about ideas.

Negative Attribute	Positive Flip Side	What's in It for You
13. Intellectually limited	Down-to-earth, practical, perhaps good body or athletic	You don't have to read Nietzsche/the *Harvard Review*/the *New Yorker*/*The History of the Federal Reserve Bank.*

The remaining work of Step Three is represented below the table, where you can match the number assigned to your partner's negative attribute in the table with a real-life example and a recommended course of action. While you should focus on the attributes relevant to your relationships, reading all of the examples and suggestions will help you to understand how, by learning from your partner's positive flip side, you can resolve your ambivalence and change the dynamic of your relationship.

ENGAGING AND LEARNING FROM YOUR PARTNER'S POSITIVE FLIP SIDE

1. *Doesn't express emotions.* This is one of the most common complaints women have about their male partners. Of course, men counter that their female partners are too emotional. Both may be right and wrong at the same time. Right because, amazingly enough, these male/female stereotypes continue to be based on reality, and wrong because, as we saw, complaining about your partner and trying to change him only reinforces the polarization. So if your partner doesn't express his feelings, rather than nag him to communicate more, learn from his calmness and logical thinking. For example, when you discuss with him an issue in your relationship, put your emotions aside and try to build a logical argument, showing him intellectually, not

emotionally, why he should consider your position. Try to be like him when he talks about "fixing" a problem, using words such as strategies, tactics, and tools.

When you lead with emotions, you trigger in him his fear of his own emotional vulnerability. So he's likely to label you "hysterical" or "neurotic" and to further withdraw into his unfeeling stance. But when you are more cognitive or intellectual, he feels less threatened and is therefore more able to emote. On his end, he should be less concerned with your "overemotionality" and more concerned with expressing his feelings. If he is more emotional, you'd feel compelled to be more logical and to articulate the thoughts relevant to the situation. In this manner you integrate more thinking into your feelings, and he, more feelings into his thinking. As a result, you no longer feel he is so emotionally uncommunicative—and bingo, your ambivalence is hardly a problem.

2. *A bad planner, irresponsible about scheduling and details, loses and forgets things.* Also a common relationship complaint by (mostly female) partners who don't recognize how they themselves collude, if not create, their partner's behavior. The best metaphor for this (but also a concrete example of it) is the backseat driver. If your partner drives too fast or misses his exits on the highway and you always correct, guide, and bug him, you only reinforce his dependence on you and his irresponsibility. What you have to do instead is let him deal with the consequences of his mistakes. True, for some time you will end up with speeding tickets, on the wrong highway, or in a dead end and, to extend the metaphor, with no milk in the house or no cash, or with the garbage piling up, or being late for appointments. But eventually he will learn from the consequences of his irresponsibility. In the meantime, instead of trying to control everything, you should learn from his ability to put his legs up and relax. For instance, leave some nonessential things for the

last minute and make some carefree, spontaneous suggestions for activities. With time you will develop a better internal balance, and as a result he will be forced to pick up some of the slack or at the very least be more responsible for his own scheduling and plans. This is not easy, I know, but if you do it you'll end up feeling less angry and therefore less ambivalent.

3. *A neatness freak, rigid, obsessive.* This is almost the opposite of type 2 above, so in trying to beat him at his own game you should try to be as obsessive, neat, and detail-oriented as possible. If you are generally a spontaneous, no-plan type, you can really learn something from his meticulous attention to details. You will become more organized and therefore more efficient, which will prevent him from occupying the entire territory of obsessive-compulsive control. The more control you exert over the details of your lives together, the more spontaneous and relaxed he will feel. Of course, this will mean more work for you and will sometimes lead to fighting, but your reward will be feeling happier with your partner.

4. *A bad dresser.* Surprisingly, this can be a major source of unhappiness in relationships. When it is, it usually means that one of the partners is unconsciously bent on looking unattractive while the other is too invested in superficial appearances. To achieve a better balance, the former needs to pay more attention to his appearance while the latter should relax his sense of style and refocus his energy on internal, intellectual, or spiritual pursuits. When this is a minor problem in the relationship, the partners can help each other to be a better dresser or a deeper thinker without needing to first address the internal lack of balance within each individual.

5. *A bit boring.* Many of my single patients dread this source of ambivalence. Not realizing that everybody becomes a bit boring after a while, they are terrified when dating someone who is not "intellectually stimulating." But in many long-term relation-

ships this can become a real problem, especially if one of the partners is a quiet, nonintellectual type and the other is an overideational type whose mind doesn't stop generating ideas and thoughts. Consistent with the general principle I'm describing, if you are the boring type, you need to develop your own mind—not to gratify your partner, but for your own growth. So read more, join a book club, or take an art history course—just for fun. On the other hand, if you are with someone who is a bit boring, you should learn from his or her stability, reliability, and contentedness. Once in a while, let your mind (and your mouth) rest and stop fantasizing about other worlds. Focus more on the immediate, concrete, and grounded concerns of your life. And again, as a by-product of this greater internal balance, your partner will be less intimidated by your intellect and more interested in developing his or her own.

6. *Introverted, quiet, not outgoing.* This sometimes comes together with type 5 above. If, even after realizing that it allows you to enjoy center stage, it still bugs you that your partner is quiet or not as outgoing as you are, you need to learn the value of silence—your own, that is. This is a simple thing to do (difficult, though, for outgoing, talkative people). If you talk less, he'll talk more, and this will work particularly well when you're with other people. Telling him to talk more will backfire as he will only feel more performance anxiety, which may well be the reason he is quiet in the first place. But being less outgoing yourself, and becoming a better listener, or at least shutting up for a while, will surely create a better balance for both of you.

7. *Critical, demanding, angry, has temper.* The specter of the explosive, angry man and the tearful, defeated woman is unfortunately familiar to any marital or couples therapist. If your boyfriend or husband is critical and angry, you need to learn from him how to be assertive and even aggressive. Feeling hurt, becoming tearful, or even withdrawing into the silent treatment

only reinforces his anger—even if it ultimately leads to an apology. This is so because unconsciously he feels empowered by your vulnerability. Your tears or even silent anger makes him feel that he has been heard, that he has impact, and he's therefore more likely to repeat the behavior. If, on the other hand, his aggression is met with yours, he finds himself in the same unpleasant place he has put you in, and he therefore has less reason to repeat it. So speak up aggressively, yell, and be critical of him. You will see that once you stop being the victim, he will stop being the victimizer. This advice, I should say, does not apply to relationships with physical aggression. While the dynamics of domestic abuse bear some similarity to our situation, the violence involved in physical conflict renders the use of this strategy quite dangerous.

8. *Restless, needs constant stimulation and ideas, wants to discuss politics/business/philosophy all the time.* Almost the opposite of types 5 and 6 above, in such extreme cases as in individuals with ADHD, this dynamic will not yield to the psychological principle of engaging your partner's positive flip side. It will still be good for you to take a page from his energy and join him in some of the activities and excitement he craves. If you do so, you'll enjoy and appreciate your partner more. But to the extent that his restlessness is caused by inborn temperament, your partner's ability to respond to your improved balance with his own is limited.

9. *Watches CNN/football/golf all the time.* How annoying when we are controlled by yet another cliché! But call it what you will, these gender-role stereotypes—which I will discuss in some detail in chapter 7—are still a source of unresolved ambivalence in many relationships. In trying to overcome this ambivalence, instead of asking him to be more like a girl, how about taking yourself to task to be more like a boy? You will see that if you start watching sports with him, sooner or later he will suggest

visiting your family or going out to dinner with friends—not simply to reciprocate, but because he needs those activities as well, and if you become more integrated, so will he. If you can't get into watching CNN/football/golf with him, learn from him to do something for yourself on your own. That too will eventually get him to initiate some joint activity of mutual interest.

10. *Doesn't make enough money.* In our society, telling your partner—especially if he happens to be a man—that he doesn't make enough money can cause serious damage to the relationship. If money is important to you, make it yourself or don't commit to someone who is not financially driven. But if you did commit to someone who doesn't make much money and you want to be happy with him, you need to adopt his values: a simple lifestyle, lots of family time at home, enjoying the basics of life, and rejecting status-related concerns. If you truly renounce your interest in materialistic things, he'll be more into them, because you will no longer express enough of this interest for both of you. If you can't—really don't want to—adopt these values, go make money yourself. In either case, when you stop expecting him to provide you with a certain lifestyle you will stop devaluing him for not delivering.

11. *A workaholic.* If your boyfriend or husband is a workaholic you're probably wondering if it's about not wanting to spend too much time with you—unless you too are a workaholic, in which case you have to question yourself as well. In my mind, a workaholic is someone who both doesn't value and avoids intimacy. While two workaholics can have parallel lives with little ambivalence about this aspect of their relationship, it is more often the case that one of the partners is unhappy about the other's workaholism. If that's your situation, complaining and nagging will only send him to spend more evenings in the office. However, if you learn from him and apply to your work or activities the same kind of single-minded drive and dedication, he might at

some point notice you're gone and come back looking for you. But as I mentioned before, this cannot be a manipulation because, in addition to the dishonesty involved, even the most oblivious of partners can smell a maneuver of this kind from any distance. It should rather be a genuine attempt to get in touch with your own need to work really hard or to escape into a compulsive endeavor.

12. *Physically not in shape.* Physical attractiveness makes a big difference, and it's hard to acknowledge this because we don't want to admit that we are superficial and because we don't want to feel limited by our body. Now however you define being in "good shape," try first to make sure that *you* are in good shape. It should go without saying that you can't expect of your partner what you don't expect of yourself, but it doesn't—as is often evident in men who demand physical perfection in their partner, their own obvious limitations in this department notwithstanding. But assuming you are in good shape and your partner isn't, what you should do is not pressure him to exercise or lose weight, but instead, learn from him how to have a more relaxed attitude about your own body. Be more accepting of your own bodily imperfections and less driven or rigid about the value of physical fitness and attractiveness. The motivation to be fit or look good has to come from *within* your partner, and it might just come if the example you provide is one of relaxation and fun, rather than of armylike basic training.

13. *Intellectually limited.* Intimate partners sometimes have different IQ levels and also different cognitive styles—one might be more conceptual, the other more mathematical, or one might be more intellectually inclined than the other. If it bothers you that your partner is not as smart, well read, or articulate as you are, learn from the positive flip side of his limitation how to be more down-to-earth, how to appreciate simple things (all universal truths are ultimately simple), or how to develop other

parts of your personality or your body. Stop being so brainy and get in shape or learn how to be kind. This will make your intellectual presentation more appealing and more likely invite your partner to emulate you. If you connect with your partner or date in these simple ways, he might stop seeing your intellect as a weapon or a divider and start thinking of it as an invitation to explore the world of ideas. The principle here, as in all the examples above, is that *if you appreciate your partner for who he is, he is more likely to be positively influenced by who you are.*

THE FINE PRINT

There is an important caveat to the technique of engaging and learning from your partner's positive flip side. The technique is based on the assumption that a relationship is like an algebraic equation, in the sense that if you change the value of one side of the equation, the other side must change as well. Putting aside the fact that relationships are not an exact science, and that therefore the analogy is imperfect to start with, to the extent that this assumption is correct—and many times it is—using this technique entails an important risk. In algebraic terms, when one side of the equation changes but the other doesn't, the equation stops working. In psychological terms, if you become more integrated but your partner fails to follow suit, your relationship—which was previously ambivalent but functional—will now likely come to an end. As an example, consider the case of a patient who was a successful, married marketing executive and a mother of two young children. Her husband was laid off from a Wall Street job several years earlier, and having been unable to find a job he ended up staying at home taking care of the children. Although my patient had a great lifestyle, a decent relationship, and two thriving kids, like many women in her position she felt torn.

She loved her job but hated the long hours and frequent business trips that took her away from her children. While her husband was really good with the kids, after some time the patient began to disrespect his passivity and lack of motivation to go back to work, and she felt resentful over his financial dependence on her.

When her oldest daughter turned five, the patient decided she had to make a change. She first talked to her husband about "switching roles," but he refused to consider any job not comparable to the one he had before, which after years of unemployment, doomed his job search before it even started. Hitting a dead end and feeling resentful and depressed, the woman got into therapy. After some time in treatment, she realized that her husband would not change and that she could only change herself. She thus worked on making a career switch to a part-time consultant, which would allow her to make a decent salary while being at home. Since her husband continued to refuse to adjust to her new priorities and look for a realistic job, making the switch meant that they would have to sell their country house, cut out expensive vacations, and lead a more modest lifestyle overall. Much to my own amazement, the patient's husband— without so much as saying so—felt entitled to their lifestyle, even without financially contributing to it. He therefore fought my patient tooth and nail about her decision, and their bitter fighting eventually resulted in separation and divorce.

So in trying to achieve more balance in her life (in a sense, to become more like her Mr. Mom of a husband), the patient unleashed a process of change that ultimately broke up the marriage. One can easily make the case, both from the children's and the patient's viewpoints, that this was a negative outcome and that the patient would have been better off not embarking on changing her side of the equation. While this may well be true from the children's perspective, the counterargument is that the outcome suggests there was serious trouble in the relationship in the first place and that the patient would be better off without her husband and potentially with another partner. But regardless of how you judge the outcome, this case demonstrates the risk to a relationship when one party undertakes to make a change in himself.

So before implementing Step Three, you might want to evaluate this risk. While you'd ultimately have to trust your instinct as to whether you think your partner would adjust, there are several indicators that could help. First, the more rigid, entrenched, or polarized the roles in the relationship, the greater the risk. In the case above, the patient was highly driven at work while the husband was completely passive with respect to his career. Second, the greater the differences in values between the partners—the husband above valued a high-end lifestyle much more so than the wife—also the greater the risk. Third, if the individual change requires significant financial or geographical changes, the risk goes up. Fourth, if substance abuse is involved—the husband above was drinking every night—the risk is substantially higher. Notwithstanding these factors, in my experience, the risk decreases significantly if the partners have a built-in, ongoing, open communication process along with a strong conviction in the value of commitment.

But the risk is always there, and because of this risk, many couples remain entrenched in Step Two. Aware of their ambivalence and feeling moderately unhappy, they don't want to rock the boat. Letting sleeping dogs lie, they don't challenge themselves or their partners, and they never get to resolve their ambivalence. This is the kind of couple whose frequent public bickering evinces a particularly bitter and tense flavor, along with a definite lack of self-deprecating humor.

4

Triangular Love

. . . she knew his cheatings!
So when she did not find him in the heaven
She said, "I am either wrong, or being wronged."
OVID

In the story of Jupiter and Io, Jupiter would only get together with his lover, Io, when his wife, Juno, was sleeping. But as an extra protection he would also spread a cloud over their meeting place on earth, so that they couldn't be seen from Mount Olympus above. One day Juno woke up from her afternoon nap and was enjoying the beautiful, clear sky. Suddenly, she noticed a thick cloud down below, which clearly didn't belong in that kind of weather. Suspecting her husband was up to no good, she rushed to check out the spot. But sensing what was coming, Jupiter managed to conceal his activity at the last minute by transforming pretty Io into a heifer. Juno, well aware of her husband's trickery, began to interrogate him about why this lovely white heifer was there. When he answered, "It just showed up," Juno called his bluff by asking for it as a present. Torn between his wish to prove his faithfulness and his love for the disguised Io, Jupiter painfully agreed to give up the heifer. Needless to say, this did not assuage Juno's suspicions, so she asked Argus, the hundred-eyed giant, to watch the heifer. Io, meantime, was suffering from her secretive, isolated entrapment, and Jupiter too could hardly bear the sorrow of watching her hurt. In the end, Io was cast away to a foreign land, and it was only when Juno finally forgave her that she got to resume her former and real shape. She then gave birth to Jupiter's son, who later in his life carried on his mother's unsuccessful bid for legitimacy.

That this story has a universal, timeless plot is self-evident. Similar story lines are indeed frequent visitors in any therapist's office. But the story's greatness is not in the plot but rather in the subtle psychological dynamics it lays out. For example, it is often the very way in which we try to conceal an affair—the cloud in the otherwise clear sky—that clues our partner to its existence. Many times this is because of unconscious guilt and the wish to be caught, which is another way of saying that the whole point of having an affair, at least unconsciously, is to triangulate—to bring a third party into the dynamic of the primary relationship. As we shall soon see, the betrayed spouse usually colludes with this, because his or her suspicious interrogations are not simply meant to establish the facts, but rather—again, unconsciously— to bring that other person, the heifer, into the marriage.

The reason couples thus triangulate—you can probably guess by now—is that they don't want to deal with their ambivalence. The husband, let's say, finds in the lover what he can't find in his wife, and in the wife what he knows he won't find in his lover. And the wife can tell herself that if it weren't for the affair, everything would be fine, meaning, she doesn't have to deal with the full picture of who her husband is—somebody who she obviously thinks is capable of lying and cheating and betraying her. Moreover, because of the rivalry with the other woman or the threat of losing her husband, the wife's desire for, or valuing of, her husband increases, and this further serves to suppress her ambivalence.

Bringing a third party into a relationship—triangulating—

doesn't always involve a sexual relationship with a third person. Indeed, the third party in Triangular Love can be a close friend, a mother-in-law, or any "extracurricular" activity that is so consuming that it appears to come between the couple. Any such third party can provide the couple with an external blame target, diverting attention from their internal ambivalence about each other.

STEP ONE: RECOGNIZING YOUR PATTERN

Because of our developmental history, emotionally speaking, we never get away from triangles. As we saw in the introduction, it all starts even before we have an actual triangle—a mother, a father, and me—in our lives (if in fact we do). In his mind, the baby creates a triangle even when he only has a two-person relationship with one caregiver, usually the mother. When the baby gets what he needs from her, she is the "good mother," and when he doesn't, she is the "bad mother." Because the infant is cognitively unable to perceive complexity and is fearful that the bad will take over the good, he divides the mother in his mind into two, literally experiencing his mother as two persons. This, according to contemporary psychoanalytic theory, becomes part of our psychological makeup, and no matter how much we grow and develop, it forever predisposes us to triangulation. If we don't get what we want from our partner, he becomes the "bad lover," and someone else, real or potential, temporarily takes on the mantle of the "good lover."

On top of that, while there are many variations and new types of families, most of us still first enter the world of love with at least the idea of a mother and a father. In this triangle, the child finds himself competing with one parent for the attention of the other. In Freudian psychology, this has a romantic component, and it results in the child's experiencing feelings of anger, guilt, and fear in relation to his rival, usually the father in the case of the boy and the mother in the case of the girl. In addition, this triangle offers further "opportunity" to divide people into good and bad or, in a more benign form of this split, to learn how to get some things from the mother and others from the father. A girl might receive empathy from her mother and soccer advice from her father, or vice versa, or she may learn the joy of board games from one parent and the love of books from another.

Understanding the developmental origins of triangulation helps us to appreciate the universal appeal of Triangular Love. It also shines a light on the two basic features that characterize all human triangles: division and rivalry. In the first we divide our own love into two, and in the second we compete with a third party for the love of our partner. Whereas within certain parameters these two aspects can have a positive impact on a relationship, when it comes to the pattern of Triangular Love, they are often quite destructive, each in its own way. And though they can certainly overlap and usually coexist in any given triangle, most of us are inclined to display principally one or the other. This is not to say that division and rivalry are mutually exclusive in any one person, and as we shall see, one can also set off the other. Nonetheless, by disposition most people are drawn more to one or the other. So if you want to stop repeating, or to prevent yourself from forming this painful pattern, your main task in Step One, Recognizing Your Pattern, is to identify the type of triangulation you are most likely to be susceptible to.

To the outside observer, or in retrospect, our role as a "divider" or a "rival" in a triangle is entirely self-evident. But while we are in the thick of it, we are often in denial. We say to ourselves, "This is so unlike me—I can't believe I'm actually doing it" or "I can't believe this is happening to me." And we often disregard the fact that it's the triangle itself, not our feelings for our love object, that fuels much of our passion.

"I never thought I would be one of those people," was the first sentence my patient Jeff, a thirty-eight-year-old Manhattan dentist, uttered, when sitting down in my office.

You see, I've been happily married, or at least I thought so, for fifteen years. I have two wonderful children and my wife, Jenna, has been my best friend ever since we fell in love, right after college. When I first met Ellen, I guess my mistress—I hate that word—she was flirting with me and I thought nothing of it. She was the dental hygienist in the practice I'm a partner in, though she'd left about a year before and got another job. And when we first became sexually involved, I told myself it was just sex, I'm not going to do it again, and I'm definitely not going to get involved emotionally. But after six months I just fell in love with her. I found myself unable to stop thinking about her, and I wanted to be with her all the time. This of course meant I was trying to get away from home more, lying to Jenna about where I was and what I was doing. I also lost interest in Jenna sexually and started fantasizing about leaving her, which really scared me. And I felt incredibly guilty and worried about Jenna's feelings if she found out, and I was always wondering if she knew. Jenna knows me really well, and she started asking me a lot of questions and a couple of times asked me, as if she was joking, if I was having an affair. Of course I lied. At the same time, I also promised Ellen that we would have a future together, even though I couldn't imagine leaving my wife and children.

Anyway, last week, about a year and a half into this, I finally told Jenna. Of course she is devastated, depressed, furious, everything. And I don't blame her—she is completely right, I acted irresponsibly and dishonestly, and I should've never started this. But I did, and my feelings for Ellen are there and I can't change them. I don't know if it can be done, but both Jenna and I want to stay in the marriage and work it out. We went to a marital counselor and he thought I should also see someone for myself, which is why I'm here.

In the next session Jeff told me his wife insisted, and he accepted, that he break off all contact with Ellen. But he told me openly that he wasn't sure he could do it. "I'm going to try, but the truth is I can't stop thinking about her, and twice I've picked up the phone to call her. One time I called and hung up." By the next session Jeff was beginning to look quite depressed—drawn face, black bags under his eyes, and a ruminating, halting speech. He said he had waited one morning by Ellen's apartment building and followed her to her job. "I didn't talk to her, but I had to at least see her," he explained. "She didn't see me."

A week later, three weeks after the breakup with Ellen, Jeff was in the throes of a major depressive episode—not eating, not sleeping, and feeling unable to enjoy anything, even his children. This depression signaled to Jeff that his love for Ellen was stronger and truer than his decision to stay with his wife. A couple of weeks later—after losing a total of twenty pounds and looking like a shadow of his former self—he talked to Jenna and the children, moved out, and started seeing Ellen again. His depression lifted instantaneously.

For some time after that, Jeff's relationship with Ellen maintained all its vitality and excitement. But after a while, the reality of their situation eroded some of the romance. His financial situation was worse, he needed to divide his time between his children—to whom he was very attached—and Ellen. And more than anything else, whereas Ellen wanted to have children of her own, Jeff was reluctant to start a second family. Of course, they knew all this was coming when Jeff left his family, but their feelings for each other were so strong that they thought love would prevail. But it didn't. They began arguing, then fighting, then developing resentments, and finally questioning their future together. And then Jeff found himself attracted to another woman.

It was at that time in therapy that the notion of triangulation started to resonate for Jeff. Before he thought that his marriage broke up because he just fell in love with another woman. But now there were more data to consider. In addition, as we revisited his relationship history, he all of a sudden "remembered" something he hadn't told me earlier in his treatment. A short time after marrying Jenna he had a "crush" on another woman, an acquaintance of theirs. While he never acted on his feelings, the crush did go on for quite a while, dissipating only when this woman moved away. And it was just then that they started a family, which drained all his extra—or extramarital—energy. This revelation made it all but evident to both Jeff and me that he was struggling with the pattern of Triangular Love. We also noted that his "most favorite triangle," or his default triangular role, was the divider, the person splitting his love into two.

Unlike Jeff, some people never realize that they tend to triangulate. They just think they keep falling in love with yet another person. Then they rationalize: in the first marriage I was too young and didn't know what I wanted; in the second my wife lost interest in sex; in the third I married on the rebound and then I really met the right woman—she just left me . . . Or they may not realize they are triangulating because it happened only once, so they attribute it to external circumstances and bad timing—meeting the right person at the wrong time, when I'm already married.

If this is your case, you must reorient yourself to think more about your internal and less about your external world. Examine or consider if something in your own unique history predisposed you to triangulate. One patient, a man in his early fifties, revealed to me that he had had three extramarital affairs. The first one started at age forty-six after twenty years of complete faithfulness. While at that time he felt his marriage had been stale, he was also aware that he was at the same age his father was when *his* affair, which led to the parents' divorce, came into the open exactly thirty-two years earlier—to the month. The patient remembered the month because it was right after Labor Day, at the beginning of the new school year that, as he put it, his world came apart at the age of fourteen. But if this was so traumatic to him as a child, why would he repeat a behavior of his father's that might well lead to the same type of divorce trauma for his own children?

The answer emerged when the patient explained that he has always blamed his dad for the divorce—because of the affair—but that looking at it as an adult, it was clear to him that his mother was depressed, flat, and therefore unresponsive and inaccessible. In other words, as a child he was never aware of his anger toward his mother and of his love for his father. He had bought into his mom's postdivorce story line that his dad was the bad guy and she the good guy. But when he was feeling in his marriage the same kind of deadness his father must have felt in his, he started having an affair, acting on, and indirectly expressing his understanding of, love for, and identification with his father. At the same time, the affair also expressed his unconscious anger toward his mother, whose apathy and inaccessibility, needless to say, had also impacted on him as a child. In other words, it was the patient's attachment to the trauma of his past—made palpable by initiating his affair at the same age and month that his father did—that blinded him to the potential trauma in his future.

For many "dividers," especially those who are married with children, the consequences of a love triangle are so painful and destructive that at some point they can't help but recognize it and therefore commit to "never again." The many marriages or long-term relationships that survive an affair fall into this category. But while "dividers" can sometimes "nip it in the bud" after one such triangular love, it is generally more difficult for the "rivals" to recognize the pattern early on. Though the consequences for "rivals" are equally devastating, it is much easier for them to deny that they have a role in the triangle. After all, if your partner had an affair, you didn't *make* him do it. And you didn't choose to be part of a triangle. At worst, you were too trusting and believed his lies even if in the back of your mind you always suspected something was going on. This is all true and you should certainly take no responsibility for his actions. But it's not the whole truth.

The prototypical "rival"—historically more likely to be a woman than a man—tells her therapist, girlfriend, mother, or a relationship advice columnist that her boyfriend flirts with other women; that her husband has no interest in sex and has been working late; that her husband told her he had some feelings for a new female "friend" and he insists on continuing seeing her; that she opened her husband's e-mail and found a personal correspondence with another woman; that she saw on his cell phone a certain number repeating and when she called it, a woman answered; that when she asked her husband if he was having an affair he just said "no" and changed the subject; that she's thinking of hiring a detective to find out if her husband is cheating on her . . .

There are endless versions to this, but the common denominator is that in the vast majority of these cases the person doesn't want to believe what she already knows and what at least to me as a therapist seems almost obvious: that her partner is involved with another person. On one level, this denial serves to postpone dealing with the pain and consequences of betrayal. In addition, it enables the "rival" to avoid facing her ambivalence toward her partner in two important ways: First, by not concluding he's having an affair, you avoid seeing something "negative" about him, that he is someone who would lie, evade, manipulate, and betray. Second, the suspicion that your partner is cheating on you evokes powerful feelings of jealousy, rejection, and abandonment, all of which highlight or fuel your passion for him. Indeed, it is a common feature of the triangle that the "rivals"—the two women or men who are involved with the same person—hold on to their love object, desperately wanting to win him over, as if he were the most valuable person on earth. If he would only be yours and yours alone, you'd be happy again. Never mind that perhaps you were not that happy with him before the affair, which may have been one of the reasons it started in the first place. Interestingly, while the rival's denial is of sufficient magnitude to allow her to avoid facing the betrayal, it's not powerful enough to reassure her that it's not going on. This paradoxical balance, which is a general property of denial, is the psychological mechanism by which the "rival" maintains an active role in the triangle.

If the "rival" is to recognize that she is in a triangle, this balance must break down. Unfortunately, because so much is invested in it, it sometimes takes months or even years for that to occur. One patient had suspected her husband was involved with a coworker for a couple of years. He would stay out late, avoid sex with her, and have long "business" phone calls on the weekends, all activities for which he provided evasive explanations. When she asked him point-blank if he was having an affair—which she did three times—he said "no," matter-of-factly, with no additions or elaborations. She accepted these responses without asking herself how it is possible that a loving husband would not be concerned with the feelings behind the question and be fine with a simple "no." And she didn't connect the dots between this and his evasive explanations of activities. It was only when he left his laptop on and she opened a suspicious e-mail to read an unmistakable erotic love letter with references to an actual sexual relationship that her denial broke down. This led to a separation and divorce, which then brought about a further breakdown of her denial, as she was now able to piece together that her husband had had two other long-term affairs during their ten-year marriage.

As I mentioned earlier, "dividers" and "rivals" are not always mutually exclusive. In fact, it is not uncommon for a "rival" to become a "divider" as a reaction to the experience of betrayal. For instance, one man in his late twenties was so devastated when he found out his girlfriend had cheated on him that he went out to a club, got drunk, and had sex with another woman. In this case, though the girlfriend "confessed" and apologized, the patient couldn't contain his anger. So he acted out in "revenge," in order to make the girlfriend feel what she had made him feel. Another patient, a woman in her late forties whose husband confessed that he had just ended an affair of two years, became clinically depressed. Though the husband was extremely remorseful and loving, she couldn't get over it and for a long time considered ending the marriage. Then, after about a year, she met a man in a bar and exchanged e-mail addresses. They eventually got together for drinks and "one thing led to another." In a few months' time, the patient—who had been married for twenty-one years and had never been unfaithful—fell madly in love with this man. Unlike the patient above, this woman, though she acknowledged that her husband's affair made it easier for her to sleep with another man, insisted that this was not an act of revenge. But with time she came to see that this was her way of getting out of the depression and that unconsciously she had aimed to reverse her husband's and her own roles in the triangle in order to come out on top.

Another version of triangulated revenge occurred in a patient who discovered that her boyfriend of six months was having long, emotional telephone conversations with his ex-girlfriend. In talking about it, the boyfriend reluctantly admitted that, yes, he still had feelings for his ex. The patient was very upset, but the boyfriend reassured her that his previous relationship was over and that he was committed to her. The patient accepted this, and the crisis abated. But a couple of weeks later, she told me she decided not to reveal to her boyfriend that one of her close male friends had been a lover in the past. Her conscious rationale was that she knew her boyfriend was possessive and she didn't want him to feel jealous. Unconsciously, however, she created precisely what she said she didn't want: when he met him or when his name would come up, the boyfriend sensed her discomfort and felt she was hiding something. In reality, there was nothing for her to hide because her romantic relationship with this man took place several years earlier, was brief, and later resulted in a completely platonic friendship. But she triangulated in unconscious revenge, creating a third person who wasn't really a threat. It was only when her boyfriend did become jealous that she realized she never really got over her own jealousy and that to "help" herself get over it she gave him a taste of his own medicine.

Among other things, this case also shows that triangulation doesn't necessarily involve sex or romance. In many relationships Triangular Love takes the form of a conflict over a best friend. Your boyfriend might feel you are spending too much time with your best friend and that she is somehow coming between the two of you. If there's truth to his claim, chances are you are using this third party to meet some of your emotional needs that are not met by your boyfriend. There is nothing wrong with this, of course, unless it becomes extreme: you end up communicating with your boyfriend only sexually or informationally, while limiting all your emotional communications to the relationship with your friend; or you confide with your girlfriend about your primary relationship, telling her feelings you wouldn't tell your boyfriend. Whereas in your perception you do this because your boyfriend is uncommunicative, in my mind you are also colluding with, and exacerbating, the problem. Rather than dealing head on with his imperfection, you are looking for the perfect partner in two people, and before you know it, you are in a triangle.

Another version of this, and perhaps one of the most ubiquitous triangles around, is the one you form when you discuss your partner's imperfections with your mother. In struggling to deal with your ambivalence about your partner, you end up creating a schism between him and your mother. This kind of triangulation is often the result of an insufficient psychological separation from one's parents—in this case, you don't accept that your primary relationship is with your partner, not your mother. Of course, your partner may resist spending time with your parents and in that way inadvertently collude in the formation of the triangle. A common if not well-understood dynamic at play here is when you become irate, critical, or contemptuous of your partner's parents for some of their personality traits, not realizing your partner shares the same traits. This is an unconscious displacement whose purpose is precisely that—to not realize that your partner has traits you don't like.

As I mentioned earlier, Triangular Love can also involve a nonhuman third party. If your boyfriend or husband is an alcoholic, chances are he is dividing his love between you and drinking, and while you might be in denial about his alcoholism, you resent having to compete for attention with his drinking buddies or his evenings out. If your husband insists on playing golf every weekend in the summer and going skiing with his friends every weekend in the winter, chances are he's avoiding dealing with what he may perceive as his boring wife. Now while you nag him and bug him to be home more, you get the "advantage" of feeling you want and need him—which you perhaps wouldn't feel if he were always there.

A similar triangulation takes place when one of the partners—usually the man—is into pornography. One young couple brought this up for discussion in their marital therapy session. The wife said she was not opposed to pornography, and her only concern was that her husband was spending too much time on Internet porn and not enough on his career goals. "I only want to talk about it in order to help him control it more, because he himself admits it can get out of control." This was a lovely, open-minded woman with an equally likable and honest husband. But notwithstanding the openness of the discussion, when I pressed the wife as to why she needed to help him control his own behavior, she admitted that it did bother her that he was turned on to such an extent by other women and that she felt threatened and even fearful that perhaps she wasn't good enough for him. The husband, on his part, said that he felt guilty about his interest in pornography and that it was therefore difficult for him to talk about it. In other words, beneath the surface, they both experienced it as a version of an affair. I will revisit this issue—the sexualization of ambivalence—in chapter 6.

DATING WITHOUT TRIANGULATING

Sometimes a triangle is just a triangle—three people or two plus an activity—thrown together by circumstances rather than by unconscious design. In these situations there's no Triangular Love to speak of, and sooner or later the temporary triangle dissolves into a successful two-person relationship. Most times, however, what starts out in triangulation is indicative of the future trajectory of the relationship. Therefore, when dating, as part of Step One, try to identify early signs of triangulation so that you can make the conscious choice to stay out of this pattern—before it even starts.

Early Signs of Triangulation

- The man you just started dating tells you he's been seeing someone for several months now but that he doesn't think that relationship is "necessarily going anywhere" and that he would like to continue seeing you. You feel you have a great connection and good communication with this man and his honesty only reinforces these feelings. You are tempted.
- You meet a wonderful, slightly older man who tells you up front he is married. He tells you his marriage is dead, he and his wife don't even have sex anymore, and they are only staying together for a couple more years until the kids go to college.
- Your boyfriend travels for business all the time and you're always frustrated and unhappy about this. He is out of town for the week, and you meet someone you're really attracted to in a bar. You ask yourself, "Why should I be lonely and a hermit while he's gone?" and you start flirting with the guy, thinking you'll end up spending the night, maybe even the whole week, with him.
- Your boyfriend of two months seems to always want to smoke weed in the evenings. He is planning long weekends away with his college buddies to Amsterdam, Las Vegas, and Jazz Fest in New Orleans. He just "confessed" to you he had a lap dance in a strip club the other night after having too much to drink. You don't mind any of these activities on their own, but your gut

tells you the whole is a greater problem than the sum of the parts.

- You've been dating a guy who you think is okay but not great. You then meet his brother, who is much cuter, and you begin to fantasize about breaking up with your guy and going out with his brother.
- You run into a guy who had asked you out in the past but you turned down. He's telling you he's seriously dating someone. He suddenly seems cool, and you feel like flirting with him and getting him to ask you out again.
- Your therapist thinks you're angry with your mom. You tell this to your mom. Your mom says therapy is not the answer. Your therapist says your mother is getting in your way.

This last item does not mean you should get rid of your therapist—or your mom. It does mean, however, that you are creating a triangle and that you should try to understand why. The most likely explanation: you are externalizing your ambivalence about Mom and about the therapist, letting them fight it out for you. To end this triangle, stop using your therapist to express anger at your mother, and vice versa. Which brings us to Step Two.

STEP TWO: UNDERSTANDING YOUR AMBIVALENCE

The shortest distance between two points is a straight line, not a triangle. So your emotional dialogue with your partner—all your reciprocal feelings, good and bad—belong in the relationship. If you tell your girlfriend "bad" things about your boyfriend that you don't tell him, and if she ends up thinking he's a jerk while you hang on to the notion that you love him so much you can't live without him, wake up—your relationship is in trouble. To generalize, a triangle almost always means the relationship is in trouble. Once you identify your "most favorite triangle" and decide to break the pattern of Triangular Love, all you have to do is to collapse your triangle back into a straight line. That is, you must work to redirect and then contain and accept your ambivalence within your primary relationship or dating partner.

To do this in a constructive way, you need to get to know and understand your ambivalence better. In my experience, there are certain types of ambivalence that put people at risk for Triangular Love. These are not the actual causes of triangulation but rather what you might *perceive or experience* as the cause. Remember, the cause is your reluctance to tolerate the ambivalence, not the specific contents of your ambivalence. But familiarizing yourself with these specific types will help you to know what feelings and thoughts you must contain within your relationship.

Type One: Lack or Loss of Sexual Interest

David was a thirty-six-year-old lawyer who had been married for ten years when he came to see me. He sought therapy because he felt he was falling in love with a coworker, a young paralegal in his firm. He was determined not to break up his marriage, so even though his coworker was also falling for him, he decided not to have an affair with her. But he kept fantasizing about her, spending time with her, and talking to her about how much they cared for each other. In short, he was in the throes of Triangular Love. When we explored his relationship with his wife, it turned out that after their first couple of years together he had lost much of his sexual desire for her. On her part, his wife didn't seem to notice or object much to the gradual decline in their sex life. As could have been expected, their sex life took a further turn for the worse after the birth of their two children, now ages six and four. So in the past several years they had little by way of sex and David had begun to feel lifeless and numb in the marriage. Clearly, David's coworker had awakened his suppressed, sleepy sexuality, making him feel once again desirable, desiring, and alive.

After a few sessions in therapy, David told his wife about me and about his feelings for his coworker. His wife got very upset and demanded he sever all contact with the other woman. Under the illusion that he could be "just friends" with the coworker, David first insisted on being able to talk to her once in a while. But after a few weeks he realized that's not what he wanted and that his sexual feelings for the woman made their friendship untenable. So he broke off all contact with her and focused his energy on trying to improve his marriage. He now entered Step Two, which was quite painful because he had to deal with his diminished sexual feelings for his wife.

David's parents divorced when he was ten. Atypically, it was his mother who left and in fact moved to another state for a while. The father's attitude to this at the time was "it's too bad, but the kids will have to get used to it." So David was unable to process or mourn the loss and instead took on his father's no-nonsense, bottom-line strategy of "moving on." Through studying this in therapy, David and I were able to see that he had basically repressed his feelings of hurt and anger in relation to his mother, but that they had returned later in life in a displaced form in his relationships with women. In two brief relationships prior to getting married he went through the same cycle of falling in love and then losing his sexual attraction. As with his marriage, the dynamic of the cycle consisted of getting close to a woman, feeling fearful of being hurt and angry over that possibility, and distancing himself through the loss of sexual interest.

In addition to understanding this history, we focused on charting how his sexual interest in his wife waned in reaction to her looking and acting more like a mother and less like a sexual object, as well as to her paying more attention to their children, the house, and her mother than to him. When we identified this, David started to act differently, implementing Step Two. He told his wife he felt that her motherhood had overtaken her sexuality, and he more directly expressed to her his anger about her not paying enough attention to him. As you might expect, David's wife was hurt and angry in return, and this resulted in a good deal of conflict in the marriage. If this sounds painful, it was. But the conflict was now *in* the marriage rather than being acted on *outside* the marriage by triangulating with a young, sexy, unmotherly third party. Also consider what happened next. First, as soon as David expressed his anger toward his wife—by arguing, pouting, or even losing his temper—he would experience a surge of sexual feelings for her. This makes sense, as he no longer needed to distance himself to express anger. Second, over time, despite her hurt and anger, David's wife actually *heard* him and decided to do something about it. She started exercising, bought some more sexy outfits, and got them a regular babysitter for Saturday nights. All this reinforced David's attraction and helped to recharge their sex life, further closing the door to potential sexual triangulation.

TYPE TWO: THE NAP SYNDROME

A patient once complained that disagreeing with one's therapist was a no-win proposition, akin to his childhood arguments with his mother about taking a nap. "It's time to take a nap," his mother would say." "I'm not tired," he'd respond. "I think you are, honey, but you just don't know it." "I'm *not tired, Mother!*" he would counter irritably, to which mother would respond, "You see, you are getting irritable, which is a sure sign of tiredness!" From my perspective, it was the patient, not me, who brought this dynamic to our relationship, "turning" me into his mother by giving me reason to offer an observation, then rejecting it while inadvertently—or unconsciously—providing further evidence to support the observation.

But it wasn't only me that the patient unconsciously hooked into this Nap syndrome. He did this with his girlfriends as well, which put him at risk for triangulation. This common dynamic is one where the girlfriend or wife assumes the position of being the nagging, controlling, and intrusive mother, while the boyfriend or husband becomes the irresponsible, passive, and unaware little boy. One man came to therapy on the verge of having an affair nine years into his marriage. "For nine years she has been complaining about my not doing this or that, not calling, not communicating, forgetting things, watching too much football, going out with the guys—you name it. She's probably right about some of these things, but I'm really sick of it and it kills my feelings for her. And now there's a woman who's really nice to me, making me feel like a man again, and I just don't think I can help it."

"So are you going to leave?" I asked. "No," he said. "I have no intention of breaking up my marriage and leaving my family. I just don't think I can help my feelings. And I know I should tell my wife about it, but I don't think I can, because she'll get real upset and she won't put up with anything like this anyway."

Because this man was never willing to stand up to his wife, he predisposed himself to eventually act out on his anger through triangulation and to have an affair. It goes without saying that he would also not tell his wife about the triangle—that would only prove she was right about him all along. And of course, he also wouldn't let go of the other woman because he wasn't ready to "act like a man." So this patient opted out of Step Two and instead terminated his treatment after a few sessions. But his reluctance teaches us about the risk of this dynamic and how to reduce it.

If you are the "child" in this type of relationship, take a nap when you're tired (i.e., do the responsible thing on your own initiative), so that if your partner keeps nagging, you have the right to get angry with her. If you are the "mother," stop telling him to take a nap so that he can have the chance to take it on his own. In other words, if you want your partner to be a man, don't treat him like a boy. And don't get devastated if he gets angry with you. You can get angry in return. If you don't want triangles, you must tolerate some conflict *within* the relationship.

TYPE THREE: THE MASCULINE-FEMININE SPLIT

In the traditional, prefeminist world, dating and relationships were polarized along conventional, rigid gender roles. In the worst-case scenario, the man was cold, calm, and logical; he was interested in sports, cars, politics, action movies, and drinking with the boys. The woman was warm, emotional, and irrational, and her interests were clothes, romantic comedies, books, and gossiping with her girlfriends. Today, while such couples still abound, men and women often struggle with the opposite dynamics: the woman is an assertive, take-charge, action-oriented type, while the man is sensitive, supportive, and emotional. When these differences become polarized, this newer version of what I call the Masculine-Feminine Split is just as untenable as the old one: the woman feels that her partner or date is a passive, submissive doormat, and the man feels that his partner is an aggressive warrior or a cold fish.

Ironically, though quite logically, the old and the new versions of the Masculine-Feminine Split create the same double trouble in relationships and dating. First, there is a deep schism in the couple's interests and therefore a lack of common ground for an ongoing dialogue. Second, there is a constant arguing and fighting over what to do and how to do it. This can set the stage for one of the partners to look outside of the relationship for someone more compatible along these basic gender roles. A woman in the traditional split may feel isolated and alienated and may eventually look for a lover who is more like a girlfriend—understanding, emotional, and vulnerable. Or a man in the newer, reversed split may feel emasculated and powerless and ultimately find a lover who is softer, more caring, and more submissive.

In my experience, the Masculine-Feminine Split is a major and universal problem in romantic relationships, and I've discussed it extensively in my book *If Men Could Talk: Translating the Secret Language of Men.* I will revisit it again in terms of ambivalence in chapter 7.

TYPE FOUR: THE BISEXUAL PARTNER

All men and women are emotionally bisexual, which is to say, they need in their partner a balance of feminine and masculine traits. But whereas in the Masculine-Feminine Split your partner might look outside of the relationship for a woman who is more feminine (or masculine) because you are too masculine or feminine, the bisexual partner looks outside for someone of his own gender. The bisexual man or woman is attracted to both men and women and feels the need for both. While this type of triangulation is not as common as the others discussed here, it is nonetheless far more common than is generally assumed. In some cases, these are gay men or women who defensively escaped from their sexuality into a heterosexual relationship, which ultimately couldn't work, because the person's gay feelings constituted a more intrinsic and authentic part of his identity. In other cases, the person might be more genuinely bisexual and triangulate because they feel a need to be with both genders.

In both scenarios, the other partner has his own reasons for triangulating, reasons that may or may not point to his own bisexuality. Also in both cases, in order to dissolve the triangle you must deal with the ambivalence toward your primary partner first. Bisexuality is often considered a torment because you are unable to sustain a love relationship with both genders, which is what you feel you need. On the other hand, you have the advantage of choosing between two appealing options.

TYPE FIVE: THE PETRIFIED PARTNER

Some people are drawn to an external love object because their primary partner is petrified, a word I use here in both of its two meanings, "fossilized" and "frightened." A partner who is psychologically underdeveloped is "stuck" at a younger emotional age. He has little by way of personal interests, conflicts, or motivations. This might be the person who mindlessly watches hours of TV every day, who is verbally inarticulate, physically inactive, and emotionally superficial—either numb or hysterical. This is also someone who is so frightened of change that he has no clue he can grow.

Since change, challenge, and even crisis are unavoidable in our lifespan, personal growth is essential to any long-lasting relationship. In successful relationships, both partners rise to the challenge and grow, separately and therefore together. But when one partner develops new interests or friendships or career goals, and the other is petrified into a mindless routine, the marriage is easily challenged by external third parties. Here too, if you are the divider you must first return to your partner and challenge him to grow—confronting him with your ambivalence head on and giving the two of you a chance to work it through. If you are the petrified partner, you must demand that your spouse accept you the way you are. After all, it's easier to grow in a judgment-free, nurturing, and supporting environment.

NONROMANTIC TRIANGULATIONS

As we saw, a couple may triangulate with a friend, a mother, drugs, alcohol, gambling, or golf, to name just a few of the common nonromantic possibilities. While I cannot address all such complex contingencies—substance abuse, for example, involves its own important dynamics of self-destruction—when it comes to a couple's life, the principle of detriangulation is the same in all cases. To find his way into a straight-line relationship, the divider in these scenarios, let's say the alcoholic, must drop his external object of attention and bring his whole self into the relationship. Once he stops drinking he might discover that he has a depressed or otherwise disengaged partner or that he himself is struggling with depression, anxiety, or sexual conflicts. With the escape route of the third-party activity blocked, he now has no choice but to face all such issues within the relationship.

Meanwhile, the other partner, the rival, who had always complained about her partner's addictive or compulsive activities but who had also perhaps enabled them so that she could avoid dealing with her own ambivalence, finds herself in an equally challenging new dynamic. She must now face such truths as her partner's anger, his trouble with monogamy or heterosexuality, his lies, or even his double life. And since he is now more fully present in the relationship, she might be confronted by her own negative feelings about him. Perhaps she was never really sexually attracted to him, or maybe she thinks he is a failure, not a nice person, too short, or whatever, but she just focused on the alcohol as the only problem. Now she too will have to express her feelings and thoughts about these issues within the relationship.

Clearly, in both romantic and nonromantic Triangular Love, "collapsing" the triangle back into a straight line can bring a new type of conflict and tumult to a couple's life. Some relationships, those that are too rigidly based on an untenable yet unchangeable status quo, do not survive this upheaval, which is perhaps just as well. Those that do survive invariably do it by venturing into the terrain of Step Three.

STEP THREE: RESOLVING YOUR AMBIVALENCE

Tolstoy wrote that all happy families resemble one another but that each unhappy family is unhappy in its own way. This might be true about couples as well, but be that as it may, it's not always easy to distinguish between happy and unhappy relationships. This is because the line between unresolved ambivalence, which is the trademark of the unhappy relationships, and resolved ambivalence, which characterizes the happier relationship, is very fine indeed.

This notwithstanding, and to stretch my geometrical metaphor to its limits, in order to overcome Triangular Love, we must resolve our ambivalence, and do it within the straight line connecting us to our partner. Accordingly, the work of Step Three consists of strengthening this line until it is fine—good—enough that it can sustain all third-party threats to the relationship.

Here, consistent with what I previously described as engaging the positive flip side, both divider and rival face the same, if separate, challenge:

- If you were a "divider" who had "lost" some of your sexual attraction to your partner, and who subsequently expressed it to her in words, not in sexual distancing, as required by Step Two, you must now reorient yourself to focus on what *is* rather than on what is *not* attractive about her. But don't fall into the trap of the artifact. For example, buying her sexy lingerie will only highlight what you are *not* aroused by. Instead, let your mind wander toward what naturally does arouse you when you're together.

- If you were a "rival" who gave up on her own sexuality and sexiness, now that you've stopped enabling your partner's extracurricular activities, refocus your attentions on the physical, sensual, and sexual. But do it for *yourself*, so that you get to feel more comfortable with your own body.

- If you've been unable to stand up to your partner and tell her to stop nagging, bugging, and controlling you, to the point that you couldn't resist falling in love (or lust) with a third party, it's time to grow up and start telling yourself, "I think I can, I think I can, I think I can," until you finally can. After the affair, don't behave like a boy who got caught and needs to be punished or to blame someone else for his transgression. Act like a man who made a mistake but who's still entitled to be treated like a man. Confront your partner when she belittles you, and take responsibility if you periodically regress into boyhood.

- Instead of believing that your man is "just another child to take care of," as many women say about their husbands, ask yourself why you structure your life in such a way that you end up taking care of someone who can take care of himself. It's precisely because he is not a child that you don't spare him your anger, frustration, nagging, bugging, and controlling. If you don't want him to play the role of the little boy, don't play the role of the mother.

- If the backdrop to your triangulation has been a polarized Masculine-Feminine Split, work on gaining greater integration within yourself, rather than focusing on your partner's gender-based imbalance. See chapter 7 for more.

- If the backdrop to your triangulation is your feeling that you have "outgrown" your partner, consider the possibility that you don't really know your partner. If he is "petrified," chances are he is not expressing to the world what's inside of him. So work on making yourself a more accepting and encouraging person so you can both find out more about his inner world.

- And if you are the "petrified partner," challenge yourself to grow so that your resistance to life ceases to collude with or even to encourage your partner's triangular adventures.

- As for the nonromantic triangulations, after acknowledging to each other your ambivalent feelings regarding each other's imperfections and problems, both you and he will need to turn inward to work on your own—not the other's—issues. In most cases involving addictions and compulsions, professional help is probably the best way to go.

BETTER LATE THAN NEVER: FROM STEP ONE TO STEP THREE IN THIRTY-FIVE YEARS

By way of demonstrating how persistent Triangular Love can be and how the three steps are integrated in real life, and perhaps in order to encourage you to confront your own pattern earlier in your life, consider briefly a patient who came to see me at age sixty-one after twenty-eight years of marriage. Arthur was a highly successful senior corporate law partner in a large New York City firm. Tall, handsome, eminently practical, and always charming, he was married to a woman who was a tenured professor of classics at a prestigious Ivy League college. Together they raised three children, all of whom were by then out of college and on various career and personal paths. Arthur loved traveling, and his wife was a wonderful cook and a great conversationalist. They always had great fun together. Nonetheless, every few years their active, joyful, and seemingly easy lifestyle would darken for some time by Arthur's unexplained bad moods, by his wife's obsessive work habits, or by their teenage children's acting up.

It all came apart after the patient's sixtieth birthday, which was a lovely, large event in an upscale New York City restaurant. It was during that party that Arthur began to wonder about his wife's relationship with one of his work partners. When the lights were out and the candles for the cake lit, he somehow sensed that his wife was a little too comfortable with the man. This triggered certain memories from previous years, for instance, when they had a party celebrating his wife's first academic book some fifteen years earlier. During that party, Arthur's then-twelve-year-old daughter came to him and said, "Mommy is kissing another man in the bathroom." At the time, aided by a drink, Arthur dismissed it as a child's misinterpretation of a congratulatory embrace.

But since his sixtieth birthday party, his suspicions about his wife and his partner continued to grow. He attempted to confront his wife, but she made him feel that questioning her about this was so ridiculous as to be out of line. However, he couldn't let go of it, so he came to see me for a consultation about his concerns. For the first couple of sessions I did nothing but listen, trying to understand what was real or imagined. But he felt so validated merely by my listening that he decided he wanted to confront his wife once again. He planned to wait a while, so he could first consider how to bring it up in a constructive way. Then one day, a colleague at work happened to mention that the partner Arthur suspected had just called him from Santa Barbara, California—the very same town where Arthur's wife was attending a three-day academic conference! This was too much of a coincidence even for Arthur—who, I was slowly but surely learning, was the master of denial. So he called his wife's hotel in Santa Barbara and asked for his partner. And what do you know, they were staying in the same hotel, on the same floor . . .

A few days later, when she returned from California (and the partner returned too), Arthur confronted his wife with his new information. The wife broke down and admitted she'd been having an affair with his partner for the past year and a half. Arthur was stunned, devastated, and angry. However, he was willing to forgive and forget if she would stop seeing her lover, which she said she would.

Sadly, even then, Arthur's denial was merely punctured, not shattered, at least until a couple of months later when he found out she was still seeing the partner. He then confronted her yet again, this time telling her she'd have to choose. This for Arthur was the culmination of Step One: facing his own denial and acknowledging what he had always sensed but never *stopped to think about lest he would have to deal with the consequences,* he came to realize that he'd been deeply embedded in Triangular Love for most of his married life. Indeed, it later came out that his wife had had two other long-term affairs, one early in their marriage with her doctoral adviser and one with a single family friend whom Arthur had always assumed was gay. Each of these affairs lasted several years, and landmarks in the development of both corresponded with Arthur's moods and/or with his children's difficulties at the time. In both cases, Arthur noticed the "unusual closeness" in his wife's relationships with these men but had somehow rationalized it to sustain his denial.

For Arthur and his wife, the end of triangulation brought about the end of the relationship, at least as they knew it. Arthur's wife did choose, by leaving him and moving in with the partner. Now Arthur felt the full weight of betrayal and it took months and months of therapy to begin to heal his wounds. During these months we also plunged into the work of Step Two, posing the central question of why he had been in such deep—actually, for Arthur it was shallow, but long-lasting—denial about his wife's affairs, which were conducted right under his nose.

The answer came loud and clear when Arthur revealed that over the years, he too had had a few "lapses" here and there, when traveling, with a legal aide and with a secretary at work. "But it was never an ongoing thing, always just a blowjob or something like that, never a relationship, and I never, ever questioned or walked away from my relationship with my wife," Arthur explained. And for a while, he insisted that while this was wrong, it was not at all equivalent to the emotional betrayal perpetrated by his wife or to her actually choosing someone else.

I told Arthur I was not interested in the question of moral equivalency but rather in whether his own triangulation played a role in his denial of his wife's, at which point he acknowledged that one of the reasons he had not confronted her in the past was his guilt over his own sexual encounters. "At the time I just felt like I didn't want to deal with all this—it just seemed ugly and unimportant. But now I know that I felt I couldn't ask her about her infidelity without talking about what I was doing." At that point, Arthur's fine legal mind also understood that his moral nonequivalency argument couldn't hold water, because even if it was true that his transgressions were less severe, they were at the very heart of his collusion with the more severe transgressions of his wife.

As Arthur's therapy continued and a few more months went by, he started dating another woman. A younger, divorced actress, this woman introduced a different kind of relationship into Arthur's life. First, whereas Arthur's wife was an intellectual, this one was a performer. She was less "in her head" and more sexual. They thus experimented sexually more freely than Arthur had done in his marriage, and in addition, unlike his wife, this woman looked up to him intellectually. Although this relationship was growing and becoming an open, loving, and intimate connection, Arthur was still thinking about his wife a great deal. In comparing the relationships, he realized that throughout his marriage he often felt his wife didn't treat him as her intellectual equal. There was a superior "I'm a more serious person" attitude to her and she somehow put down his profession, considering it an uninspired, lesser choice. With my help, Arthur now began to see that his extramarital sexual encounters were all with women he considered "lesser," and that this was his way of unconsciously (1) feeling better about his masculinity and (2) expressing his anger with his wife for making him feel emasculated. In other words, in order to not bring painful, angry feelings into the relationship, he periodically "exported" them sexually, through a third party. With these realizations, Arthur further deepened his Step Two work, which at this point was taking place not in his relationship but rather in his mind. That notwithstanding, this work suggested that he had never fully let go of his wife and that in a sense he was still triangulating, and to the extent his wife was also still thinking of him, they were now involved in a square . . .

Amazingly, this turned out to be the case. Just as he was getting ready to move in with the girlfriend, Arthur's wife contacted him. It turned out that while living with her lover, she too got into therapy, engaging in her own Step Two, realizing that her extramarital affairs were a reenactment of a forbidden childhood sexual experience—really abuse—with her older brother. As they discussed this in a long afternoon walk in Central Park, Arthur revealed his own sexual secrets as well as his new insights about their relationship. By sunset it was clear to both of them that their relationship was far from over. They decided they would both break up with their lovers and get into marital counseling, while still living apart, to work on their relationship. They did so, and over the next six months, with the help of a marital therapist, they talked about everything they didn't talk about for twenty-eight years: anger, sex, guilt, insecurities . . . *Everything* was on the table.

They were now working on Step Two together, with a new line of communication, which for the first time in more than thirty years included arguments, fights, depressing dead ends, and painful revelations. But there were no inexplicable moods, secrets, lies, guilt, and denial. Furthermore, when the fights subsided, there would be an immense pleasure in the richer intimacy of their interactions and in their greater sense of self-and-other acceptance. I've never before seen such a transformation of a relationship: from Step One to Step Two it was as if it were a different relationship.

Perhaps because of the magnitude of this change, Step Three presented itself somewhat less dramatically. When Arthur and his wife moved back in together they continued their work in individual therapy, where they were able to use new insights to engage the positive flip sides of their partner's troubling attributes. For instance, after repeatedly confronting his wife about her intellectual arrogance, Arthur was able to see that some of his anger in this area had sprung out of his own intellectual insecurity, not just his wife's arrogance. So in order to overcome his insecurity, he borrowed a page from her world and signed up for an online course on James Joyce, eventually writing a unique critical essay on *The Portrait of the Artist as a Young Man* and submitting it to important literary magazines. He also started writing philosophical short stories, developing his interests in literature and the nature of thinking.

At the same time, Arthur's wife began to understand something about her own need to devalue her husband's intellect and to look for exciting sex elsewhere. As a result, she now appeared to be learning from Arthur's more down-to-earth, practical approach to things, including sex. She was therefore able to feel more sexually comfortable and experimental within the frame of her primary relationship. Gradually, this type of individual yet reciprocal work on the part of both Arthur and his wife served to reduce the frequency and intensity of their fights. It also increased their sense of mutual acceptance and belonging, which basically eliminated the threat of Triangular Love from their lives.

It was indeed remarkable to see how, after so many years together, this couple virtually reinvented themselves. Having traveled through years of triangulations, complete with deceit and denial, they stepped into a brave new dynamic consisting of straightforward confrontation, to finally reach, only in their later years, the fine line of communication in which negative feelings are not merely expressed but also integrated into the relationship.

5

Forbidden Love

And then they would scold the wall:
'You envious barrier,
Why get in our way?'
OVID

The story of Pyramus and Thisbe was the basis for Shakespeare's *Romeo and Juliet.* In the Greek myth, the two youths live next door to each other and their parents forbid their love. But as Ovid put it, "Fire suppressed burns all the fiercer" and "Love is a finder, always." So the two lovers find a way to communicate—through a crack in the wall. Then, as their desire and frustration only continues to grow, the youths decide to defy the barriers to their love and run away from home. However, their plan to meet at night by the mulberry tree is foiled by an ironic twist of events resulting in their tragic death.

While not nearly as tragic, the Forbidden Love to be explored in this chapter also cannot be materialized. When the lovers attempt to bring their secret relationship into the light of day, love, if not the lovers, will die. And the consequences to their lives may indeed be tragic, in the sense that in vying for more they end up with less and in seeking freedom they end up with more chains. Historically, Forbidden Love can be viewed as one that simply defies culturally dependent norms of behavior. Clearly, as

Western civilization continues to broadly progress along a socially liberal trajectory, many of yesterday's forbidden loves are no longer forbidden today. Others, such as interracial dating in America, might not be explicitly forbidden—except by some on the cultural margins—but might still be tacitly censured.

But no matter how liberal we are, we cannot escape the sense that romantic love rather easily evokes an intrinsically forbidden element. Extreme cases—like that of a schoolteacher who is impregnated by a thirteen-year-old student and then continues to see him despite repeated warnings, legal action, and jail time—periodically make it into the media. Less dramatic cases, such as the college student and her professor or the married man and his children's au pair, are obviously more common. In all these cases, Forbidden Love clearly overlaps with some of the other patterns I've discussed, for example, Triangular Love. Nevertheless, the forbidden aspect of love and the specific role it plays in many relationships is important enough to merit its own discussion.

To the psychoanalytic therapist, the notion that love may be intrinsically forbidden is hardly news. If you are a Freudian, it all goes back to your first erotic love object—the parent of the opposite sex—who is dangerously out of bounds. But you don't have to be a Freudian to see that love can in fact be dangerous in the life of a family. There's little question that parents and their children fall in love with each other, with the nearly universal caveat that in this context separates love from sexuality. But aren't these two inherently close in nature, sometimes evoking each other and looking to intersect? For example, as preposterous as it sounds, isn't it theoretically natural for a brother and sister to be attracted to each other when they reach puberty? And in general, isn't it to be expected that the intimacy of family life would trigger sexual feelings in its members? Well, the fact is, incest does exist, which is precisely why it's such a taboo.

Indeed, notwithstanding sex education and progressive family environments in which sexuality is mentioned as a "beautiful and healthy" part of adult love, in most families, nudity, arousal, and sex are nowhere to be seen, heard, or spoken. At the same time, sexual references are ubiquitous everywhere else in our culture, stimulating even further the child's existing curiosity and imagination. In other words, you don't need to be a psychologist to see that children in our society grow up with the notion that sexual love is exciting and wonderful and at the same time forbidden—at least for them.

STEP ONE: RECOGNIZING YOUR PATTERN

Kim came to see me when at the age of thirty-three she realized there was something wrong with her relationships. She had one four-year relationship that she tearfully and movingly described as open, mature, loving, and just wonderful. But since it ended some three years ago, she hadn't met anyone as exciting, loving, and available. She has had a few short-term relationships, but they lacked the connection she felt with Christopher and went nowhere. When I asked her why she and Christopher didn't work out, she started crying again and said, "He wasn't Jewish."

Kim was not a practicing religious person, but she grew up in a traditional, conservative Jewish community and it was always her intention to marry a Jewish man. When she met Christopher she was twenty-six and she didn't think it was going to be serious. But as their feelings for each other grew, she told Christopher—and herself—that she could never marry him. For a while she wondered if he would convert, but he was a church-going, if not a fully practicing, Catholic, so she knew, and he confirmed, that it was not an option.

Therefore, after a few months of dating they decided to stop seeing each other. But this broke their hearts, so they continued to talk on the phone, which led to getting together for lunch, which led to dinner . . . and so on. They were soon back together, and as Kim described it, they had an ideal relationship full of passion and compassion. But all along they both knew that "one day" they would have to break up. In addition to her own conviction about wanting a Jewish life, Kim was very close to her mother and she felt that marrying a Gentile would "kill her."

As Kim perceived it, Christopher was very sensitive and kind and he understood where she was coming from, therefore never pressuring her. "We were so much in love, and so happy together, that we didn't want to break up. We actually tried again, twice, but each time we parted crying, saying we can't do this, and then after a few days or a couple of weeks we got back together."

Finally, when Kim turned twenty-nine, her mother introduced her to a friend's son, a Jewish accountant, who immediately wanted to date her. Kim told Christopher about this and he was devastated, thinking she was on her way to marrying this man. Kim thought so herself, so she and Christopher broke up yet again and she started dating the accountant. However, after a couple of months, Kim realized that she couldn't muster any feelings for this man. She broke it off, and she then tried to re-contact Christopher. But she couldn't reach him, and she soon found that he had left the country and was traveling around the world. Stunned and pained, Kim was at last beginning to see that this chapter in her life was coming to an end. But it wasn't until she reopened the wound in therapy that she was able to more fully understand the relationship and let it go. You see, while she had previously thought that if it weren't for the fact that Christopher was Gentile they would have been together and married, after some time in therapy, she came to realize that if it weren't for that fact, they wouldn't even be together in the first place—at least not for as long as they were. Not only was their love made sweeter, more fervent, and more intense by its forbidden element, but it was also "powered" by a forbidden theme in Kim's history.

Kim's father died when she was a young girl and her mother never remarried. Kim was an only child and she and her mother were extremely close, so much so that she felt she never missed having a father—she felt completely loved and cared for by her mother. However, as she quickly discovered in therapy, her closeness to her mother was contingent on her being a well-behaved, mature, and responsible girl rather early on. Along with this came an enormous sense of admiration, gratitude, and obligation to her mother for doing such a great job raising her all by herself. As a teenager, she was interested in boys but basically avoided dating because she was so close to her mother that she didn't really feel the need to go out. "I guess I also thought it would upset her if I had boyfriends, being that she was alone and unmarried." The more we explored Kim's relationship with her mother, the more it appeared that, to a large extent, their closeness rested on a not-too-uncommon mother-child role-reversal syndrome: Kim was unconsciously taking care of her mother's emotional needs.

As a part of this role reversal, Kim had suppressed any feelings of separateness, even as a teenager, where one's quest for autonomy often takes on a rebellious, oppositional form. But not in Kim. For her, rebelling openly would have evoked too much guilt. So she continued to be a good girl until her need to separate and get on with her own life was no longer resistible. However, when at the age of twenty-six she finally attempted to transfer her emotional dependency from her mother to a boyfriend, Christopher, Kim could not do this "out in the open" as a natural developmental step. So she unconsciously picked a forbidden nonstarter who ultimately wouldn't take her away from her mother. From this point of view, Christopher could have been any run-of-the-mill unavailable man. But selecting a love object who is forbidden not only to herself but also, and perhaps more to the point, to her mother allowed her to finally rebel.

Given her enmeshment with her mother, the only way to separate was to break the rules—in this case the cultural, religious rules she was raised with. Of course, she didn't truly rebel, as in defying her mother—and the mother within—by marrying a Gentile. This was still too dangerous. Instead, the teenager within her gathered all her denied and repressed emotional needs and channeled it into the poignant longings and secret thrills of Forbidden Love. Surely, discovering Christopher and intimacy with a man, as well as unconsciously searching for an absent father, also played a role in her passion. But more than anything else it was her search for freedom and individuality in unconscious teenage rebellion against her mother that determined her choice of Christopher.

Interestingly, as distinctive as this circumstance in Kim's history was, the nearly overpowering appeal of Forbidden Love almost always involves a teenagelike rebellion. This is because it's in adolescence that we enter adult sexuality with the implicit threat of separating ourselves from our childhood and our parents, *even though we are not fully ready for it.* Indeed, parents (and society at large) are threatened by adolescent sexuality precisely because it signifies the teenager's attempt to break away from parental control. So if you find yourself, like my patient, Kim, in a Forbidden Love relationship, Step One, Recognizing Your Pattern, requires that you recognize that it is your own rebellion—conscious or unconscious—more so than your connection with the other person that fuels your passion.

Now rebellion against social conventions is not necessarily a bad thing. If you are gay, should you accept religious or cultural prohibitions against pursuing your love object? Of course not. If you are a white woman dating a black man, should you consider this Forbidden Love, if, say, your family or others in your society don't approve? Once again, no. How about a young woman dating an older man? Again, I would say no, though in all of these instances it all depends on your own intellectual and emotional attitude toward these social conventions. If, as an independent thinker, you embrace your rebellion and commit to your love, it's clearly no longer forbidden. On the other hand, if you claim to be free but act like a grounded teenager who secretly or subversively enjoys breaking the rules, chances are you are under the influence of Forbidden Love.

As evidenced by Kim's case, getting to Step One in Forbidden Love can be quite difficult. First, the depth and range of feelings brought into such a relationship is often extraordinary. This is not typically recognized by an outsider who is too busy condemning the relationship for breaking the social norm. Yet, as any lover of literature would confirm, when invited to the inner world of Forbidden Love by a novelist, we are often moved to identify and sympathize with the protagonists. We do not read or sit through *Romeo and Juliet* saying to ourselves, "Oh, they are such teenagers." My personal favorite of this type of artistic catharsis comes from the opera world. Whatever we think about brother-sister incest—indeed, regardless of the terrible psychic damage it brings about when it occurs in the real world—Wagner's musical depiction of such love in *The Valkyrie* places the listener completely on the side of the lovers. Their famous love duet, culminating with "Du bist der Lenz, nach dem ich verlangte in frostigen Winters Frist" ("You are the spring for which I longed in frosty winter time"), is one of the most tender, harmonious, and passionate pieces of music ever written.

THE TEENAGER WITHIN OR TRUE LOVE?

This is what Kim felt in relation to Christopher, which is why it took her four years to break up the relationship. In addition to having to resist this kind of emotional depth, and yes, beauty, getting to Step One is also difficult because we view the reality of the obstacle (i.e., wrong religion, gender, age, marital status) as entirely external and objective rather than as partly created by our own perception and reluctance to legitimize our love. So how to know whether you are guided by the "teenager within," which you should outgrow, or by true love, which you should embrace? Well, as with the other failed patterns of love, sometimes you just "have to be in it to win it." In other words, the only way to know is to fully reject those external obstacles and to fully commit to your love. If the love then dies, you know it was only fueled by rebellion. If you choose not to test it out, meaning, you continue a relationship that you know remains ul-timately unacceptable to you or to your partner, then by defini-tion you are engaging in the pattern of Forbidden Love. The same is true if you pursue the relationship in secret in order to avoid social or familial disapproval.[1] This logic makes it quite

---

[1] This discussion raises an important issue relative to the lives of many—especially young—gay men and women, who feel they must hide their love life in order to protect themselves or their partners from such real external threats as social rejection, discrimination, or even violence. Arguably, whenever possible, gays in this situation should strive to come out where they can, at least to a small group of close friends. Hopefully, they can bring their secret into the open to a more or less accepting environment or subgroup or else perhaps move to a more accepting community. While this can be a real struggle—a struggle that some of my gay patients have indeed traversed for many years—it is one worthy of con-sideration. For without it, understandable as their choice may be, they are bound to feel illegitimate, which means their relationships can't help but be infected by the dynamics of Forbidden Love.

simple, at least in theory, to ascertain which dating situations you should avoid if you wish to stay clear of Forbidden Love. For example, if you know you would never *marry* outside of your religion, don't *date* outside of your religion. If you know you would never have a relationship with a married man (or colleague or boss), don't go out for drinks with one.

These examples can be generalized to an equation that fits all possible scenarios: If you know that you would never break (your own) rule X, don't even bend it by dating person Y if committing to him is forbidden by X.

Obviously, this formula requires "knowing" that you "would never" do something—and can anyone ever really know that? Nonetheless, the more you know yourself, the more likely you are to avoid dating someone you consider forbidden. If you are not sure whether a particular person is forbidden for you, perhaps the following hypothetical test question would help. Imagine being married to this person, having a family with him, and what your relationships with your family of origin, his family, your friends, and his friends would be like. You can use this exercise regardless of your age or where you are in life, and even if you never want to get married. The idea is to get a picture of a public commitment that *you* can live with. So in this scenario, regardless of whether other important people in your life would react positively or negatively to your choice, would you still choose it? If your answer is yes, chances are that this person is not forbidden based on your own inner values.

Finally, what about the possibility of love triumphing over "inner values" that are based on ignorance and prejudice, in which case, after getting to know your partner and realizing how much you want to be with him, you renounce the social norms that had made him initially forbidden? This is a distinct possibility that provides an important exception to the general rule above. As I said, sometimes we can only find out about the nature of our patterns by further engaging in them.

STEP TWO: UNDERSTANDING YOUR AMBIVALENCE

If you think back to your college years or perhaps midtwenties, you might be able to recall a specific moment when you suddenly realized not so much that you are free of parental supervision but rather that in the absence of that supervision you must now create your own internal supervisor. Perhaps it was the first time you learned how to budget or how to say no to yourself, whereas before your parents were the ones to do it. This type of moment represents true freedom. Not freedom *from* something, as in freedom from parental supervision and its concomitant escape into rebellion, but rather freedom *of* something, as in freedom of choice, which is wholly contingent on our capacity for self-supervision.

This concept is at the heart of Step Two, Understanding Your Ambivalence, in which you make a choice and accept the consequences. Having identified your pattern of Forbidden Love, your job now is to develop a sense of boundary, an internal wall that will protect you from the forbidden. DON'T GO THERE, the sign on the wall says, pointing to what *you*, not your parents or society at large, consider forbidden. The territory of the "not forbidden," or acceptable defined by this wall, may be smaller or bigger than the terrain you've trekked in the past. For example, a relationship with a married man may now be excluded, or a relationship with a man of a different race may now be included. This wall within is not simply a set of rules but rather an evolving psychological structure whose mission is to contain, and at some point perhaps even to replace, the teenager within. As you might expect, this emerging function thrusts you right into the land of ambivalence. Let me illustrate.

One patient started his therapy, consistent with how he grew up, as a religious, modern orthodox Jew. He came to see me in his late twenties after breaking up a long-term relationship with a like-minded, totally kosher woman because he was not ready to get married. He had little by way of other relationships and therefore felt he couldn't settle down before dating some more. But it turned out that the dating experiences he subsequently sought out were almost always forbidden. First he dated a woman whom according to some truly obscure biblical decree having to do with his and her family history, he was not allowed to be with. For a while he rationalized this by avoiding inter-course with her, which of course made it all the more desir-able. Eventually, after consulting with his rabbi, he concluded he didn't need to abide by this rule, as it was apparently adhered to only by ultraorthodox Jews. So he consummated the relation-ship. But some time later he lost interest and broke it off.

He then stopped dating for a while but became involved in a highly charged sexual relationship with a woman who was not looking for "a relationship." There was an understanding be-tween the two that this was strictly casual with no strings at-tached. This nonrelationship paralleled a change in the patient's religious orientation. Though he continued to feel very much identified with Judaism, he began to question his faith and even stopped wearing his yarmulke. Nonetheless, this relationship felt forbidden to him because he completely objectified his partner, treating her in his mind as a sex toy—albeit a consenting one—rather than a human being. So after a year of struggling with his guilt, he broke this off too.

For the next couple of years he tried to date but couldn't find anyone who really excited him. But then he found himself being attracted to and pursuing younger, non-Jewish women. At this point he and I finally came to see that even though he had continuously expanded the territory of the acceptable for himself, he was still looking for relationships outside the wall. Whereas by this time he was no longer practicing religion, there was still no doubt in his mind that he would only marry a Jew. So what was he doing pursuing those noncandidates? Was he still not ready to settle down, even though by now he was in his midthirties? No, he was ready all right. But the women who were in his mind "marriage material" (i.e., Jewish professionals in their late twenties or early thirties) were not as sexy. Or they were too needy or too controlling or too . . . motherly.

Simply put, and ignoring other important variables, these more eligible women reminded the patient of his mother, whom in childhood he had experienced as an overprotective (i.e., needy plus controlling) parent and from whom he had always struggled to separate. So in pursuing Forbidden Love the patient had been trying very hard to avoid his ambivalence, which consisted of perceiving women who were caring, responsible, and mature— all qualities he valued—as nonsexual, needy, and controlling. Indeed, there was little risk of having to deal with these qualities in young, sexy, unacceptable, or otherwise intrinsically forbidden women.

Once we figured all this out, the patient was able to reach Step One and say no to his teenage self. He was then able to form a relationship with a Jewish woman who was about his age and who was completely kosher by his own definition. For the first time since he started therapy, he was in a relationship with an equal whom he loved and respected and with whom he had an open dialogue and a basic compatibility in culture, values, and sensibilities. This was highly gratifying for him but also quite a challenge, because he struggled with what he perceived as his girlfriend's dependency on him. It bothered him that she wanted to spend more time together than he did, that she wanted to talk on the phone more, that she wanted to "talk about the relationship" more, and that sexually she was not as exciting as some of the other women he had been with. Eventually, the relationship failed because both partners were unable to transcend this dynamic. But at least the patient had the experience of Step Two, which allowed him to struggle with ambivalent feelings in a relationship that fell within the territory of the acceptable, as marked, for the first time, by his own, self-imposed boundaries.

SLEEPING WITH THE ENEMY

Another example, perhaps a more successful one, comes from a black, gay patient who was in a long-term relationship with a white man. For a long time this was a forbidden relationship for my patient not because it was a gay relationship, but rather because being with a white partner was unacceptable in his social circle. The patient's cultural milieu was the black ghetto where he grew up and a close-knit network of black friends, most of whom felt that he had "sold out" by "sleeping with the enemy." During that time my patient would either argue with his friends about this or, alternatively, minimize the significance of the relationship and hide from them the extent of his involvement. While this created tension in his friendships, it did have a psychological "advantage": the patient didn't have to face his own uncertainty about his choice. When you are ambivalent or conflicted about something and someone else takes a side, you take the other. In other words, since his friends were "holding" or representing all the negative feelings about being with a white boyfriend, it was natural for the patient to argue for, and be more in touch with, the opposite position. In addition, as is often the case, the public designation of the relationship as forbidden only served to fuel his private passion for it. So as a result of these dynamics, the patient didn't have to be conscious of his own ambivalence.

After a while, though, he decided he was no longer willing to live with Forbidden Love. For him, Step Two meant embracing the relationship more fully and challenging his friends to accept it. He decided to move in with his boyfriend and they bought an apartment together in an upper-middle-class neighborhood, which, as he expected, provoked even more rebuke from his friends. Now he was a bona fide Uncle Tom. But his new public commitment to the relationship legitimized it in his own eyes and forced his friends to deal with it. He told them that he needed their support but would not accept their bigotry, and this further diminished the forbidden aspect of the relationship. While most of his close friends accepted the relationship, a couple didn't, and as a result those friendships ended.

Now that he was no longer in a forbidden relationship, the patient had to deal with his own—you know what—ambivalence. No longer hiding from or fighting the opposition, he had no choice but to feel his own sense of loss, sometimes even regret, that he was with a partner who could never really understand his experience of growing up black in the inner city, or even of being black now, facing constant, if subtle, discrimination. As a consequence, there was now more conflict in the relationship itself. For example, an angry fight erupted when the patient described how he felt he wasn't being promoted as fast as other people in his company, perhaps because of his race. The boyfriend's instinctive reaction was to doubt that race was the reason, which made my patient wonder if his friends were right after all. But he hung in there, facing his conflicts with his boyfriend and dealing with his own ambivalence.

To generalize, as we say no to ourselves in Step Two we have to be able to deal with loss: either the loss of adolescence—

defined here as the end of freedom for subversive rebelliousness—or the loss of being with a partner who in some important way is quite different from us. The latter form of loss, it should be noted, is to some extent true about any relationship we commit to.

STEP THREE: RESOLVING YOUR AMBIVALENCE

Taking a walk in an affluent American suburb you will sooner or later encounter, on one of the manicured front lawns, a well-groomed dog, raucously barking at you. Rushing toward you, yearning and imploring to come out and play, the dog, though certainly not his barking, is suddenly brought to a stop, as if held back by an invisible barrier. In fact, this dog *is* being held back by a so-called invisible fence, and a device on his collar subjects him to an electric shock when he tries to cross the property line.

In many a relationship, one or both parties are likewise invisibly fenced to the relationship or marriage. Bound by fear of the consequences to themselves rather than by a sense of one's own free will, they never or rarely stray and as a result do not appear susceptible to the pull of Forbidden Love. As in the case of the dog yearning to play with strangers in the street, however, the threat of consequences only serves to reinforce and enhance the forbidden desire. These relationships, therefore, are in a sense stuck in Step Two. No longer a teenager, you now live in a prison of your own making.

The idea of Step Three, Resolving Your Ambivalence, is to liberate ourselves from this doglike, social-contract-based dynamic. If in Step Two we say no to Forbidden Love because we believe it is indeed forbidden, in Step Three we say yes to our relationship by understanding that *Forbidden Love is in fact not forbidden after all.* We accept our relationship for what it is, as is, and stop longing to jump over a fence that is not invisible but rather nonexistent. This, admittedly, is a tall order. But it's a basic requirement for a happy monogamous relationship.

One of my patients, Donald, truly believed in the ideals of commitment and monogamy and would have never gone into therapy if it weren't for the crisis that challenged these beliefs. Married for nearly twenty years, Donald had four children. He came to see me because he had fallen in love with another woman, a broker named Alice who had worked for him in his real-estate business. He described his feelings for this woman in caring, respectful terms, saying repeatedly that more than anything else she was a wonderful friend. She was married as well, and while they acknowledged their attraction to each other, they had refrained from acting on it sexually. Nonetheless, Donald was panicked because he felt that if she'd be willing to leave her husband, he would leave his wife and break up his family for her.

But while this panic made him realize he needed help, there was no quick fix on the horizon. For one thing, his feelings for Alice made him feel once again alive, inspired, and motivated. He was excited to go into the office every day, looking forward to their long lunches and occasional afternoon walks in the city. During this time, neither Donald nor Alice brought up the question of their future together. For Donald, this in itself produced an incredible sense of excitement and tension: every day he would go to work both hoping and dreading that she would bring it up and say she would leave her husband for him. This bittersweet torment, combined with the more obvious behaviors of secrecy and deceit—Donald had to work some on concealing his whereabouts during the workday from his wife—is typical of Forbidden Love.

After some time in therapy I confronted Donald with the observation that longing for freedom while at the same time hiding it from an authority figure—he had clearly turned his wife into one—was the hallmark of teenage rebellion. Viewing himself as a responsible, mature person, Donald didn't like hearing this. But he knew it was the truth and he decided to accept it, thereby bringing himself to Step One. In behavioral terms this meant that he finally broke his and Alice's code of silence about the future. Knowing full well that by bringing it up he was drawing a close to the state of psychic suspense fueling his longings, he asked Alice if she would ever consider ending her marriage. Alice said no, she couldn't imagine that, even though she thought about it every day. Feeling relieved, Donald immediately realized that when push came to shove, he wouldn't walk away from his marriage either. Of course, he wasn't really tested because Alice had said no. On the other hand, unlike many people in his situation, he had never actually consummated the affair with Alice.

Next, Donald had to deal with the secrecy aspect of his Forbidden Love. He told his wife, Elena, that he had "developed feelings" for a woman at work, and he told Alice that he wanted to just be friends, the kind who talk to each other every couple of months. Elena wisely said it was up to him to resolve it, and Alice, also wisely, accepted his decision. Amazingly, all three agreed that it wouldn't be right for Donald to terminate Alice's employment—which he could have found a way to do—even though it would have made it less painful, at least for Donald and Elena. These actions, though by no means as simple or smooth as implied in my account, set in motion an irreversible process separating Donald from his Forbidden Love. Initially Donald only minimized his work contact with Alice, but with time, as their feelings for each other dissipated, they stopped even talking. Eventually Alice left the job and completely disappeared from Donald's life.

But this was not the end of Donald's troubles. In addition to having to work on regaining Elena's trust and on healing her wound, he now had to start dealing with the marital problems that had predisposed him to Forbidden Love in the first place. So here we go again: try as we may, there's no escape from ambivalence. In Donald's case, while he was very close and connected to his wife, it bothered him that she was physically not in great shape, that she didn't have her own career or "outside" interest, and that she didn't appear as strong or as independent as some other women. So in Step Two Donald had to accept all this. He did so, with my help, by (1) repeating to himself every day for some time, "There's no other way, there's no other road"—remembering, of course, that he, the adult, not the teenager within, had made the choice to stay in the marriage; and by (2) exploring why Elena's *particular imperfections* had bothered him so much.

This second point led us to—where else?—his childhood. It turned out that his mother, who grew up in rural northern Michigan and never really adjusted to life in the big city, was, as he put it, "emotionally weak." She had many fears and therefore never drove, swam, or exercised. And her feelings were always rather easily hurt. Finally, she was needy and dependent, not only in relation to her husband but also to her firstborn child and only son, Donald. So having been exposed to this kind of feminine care, Donald couldn't stand having a wife who reminded him, even slightly, of his mother. As for Elena's being a little overweight, this made her seem more motherly in general, which didn't help matters. Now, however, by redirecting the intensity of his ambivalence to where it belonged in the first place—his mother—Donald was better able to accept and live with his imperfect marriage, without having to resort once again to Forbidden Love.

At this point, with an acceptable, tolerable marriage, one cannot help but think of Freud's notion that the purpose of psychotherapy or psychoanalysis is to turn neurotic symptoms into common unhappiness. Now, if you're reacting to this with contempt or disgust, feeling that a "tolerable marriage" is just not good enough, well, I agree. As a matter of fact, this state of affairs could have taken Donald back to where he started—looking to replace everyday marital misery with extramarital love. So accepting his ambivalence was not good enough for Donald. He needed also to deal with it. In the past he avoided dealing with it because he didn't want to hurt his wife's feelings, so he had never told her about his reservations. But now, in giving up on the wish for *another* woman, he allowed himself to experience and express his feelings about *this* woman and, in particular, his unhappiness about her weight and dependency needs.

Naturally, this was painful for Elena to hear, especially on the heels of his betrayal, but it also gave her a chance to consider her own feelings about her imperfections. She could have said, "That's your problem, I'm happy with who I am and I don't want to hear anything about this," which would have been completely legitimate. But this was not what she really felt. In truth, she herself was unhappy with her weight and dissatisfied with her lack of independent direction in life. So although she did get hurt and angry, she also acknowledged these feelings and subsequently started exercising and exploring various job opportunities. Eventually, she went back to school, got a master's degree in education, and developed a successful career in online educational consulting.

Expressing his frustration and anger—valid or invalid as it may have been—was Donald's attempt to deal with his ambivalence. While this is often a risky strategy, the fact is, many long-term relationships are stuck in a low-level, chronic unhappiness because the partners are afraid of conflict. They may intellectually accept their partner's imperfections in the sense that they say no to external temptations, but they avoid the intimacy of full honesty, thereby foregoing the opportunity to go through a conflict and come out on the other side with a deeper, emotional acceptance of their partner. This touches on the basic non-Freudian psychoanalytic understanding of Forbidden Love: because we are afraid that our anger will destroy our love for the "object" (originally mother or other primary caregiver), we avoid expressing it openly, instead doing it by means of a subversive rebellion. In Forbidden Love, this choice becomes self-reinforcing as we end up resenting our primary partner even more because he or she stands in the way of our new love and on top of that also makes us feel guilty. We must therefore suppress our anger all the more. Our forbidden partner, on the other hand, is perceived by us as a victim of circumstances who can do no wrong. We thus achieve our psychic goal of separating love from anger but further distance ourselves from our relationship goal of having real and lasting intimacy.

Now if expressing negative feelings, hopefully with a constructive intent, is a necessary condition for a successful relationship, it is hardly a sufficient one, which brings us to Step Three in Donald's therapy. Here, Donald had to understand that he was a prisoner not of his marriage or relationship but rather of his own psychology, past and present. Specifically, when he was thirteen, his father left the family and Donald was suddenly thrust into being the "man of the house." Not only did he have to emotionally support his distraught, worried mother, but he also had to help her raise his two younger sisters. He would supervise their schoolwork and babysit for them so that his mom could work a couple of evenings a week to earn some badly needed cash. Donald was a conscientious and responsible teenager, and to an extent he also enjoyed his new position in the family. But of course he also resented the situation and he resolved to not repeat his parents' mistakes, financially or emotionally.

Determined to make and save money, Donald worked

through both high school and college. He later went to business school and ultimately started what would become his own rather successful real-estate brokerage. At the same time he desperately wanted to have a stable, "unbroken" family life, so he married his college girlfriend, Elena, right after they graduated. As we explored this history in therapy, it became evident that Donald's problem was nothing other than this very success: he achieved all of his objectives, all too soon. In other words, he suffered from an early foreclosure of his adolescence. Aiming for stability and security at a young age, he didn't have the opportunity to explore, play, and experiment. Consequently, later in life he felt imprisoned by what he perceived—with some objective justification—as his irreversible early adulthood decisions.

Now whereas Donald's initial crisis stemmed from the conflict between his early determination to avoid repeating his parents' mistakes and his self-perceived need to free himself from the limitations of marriage, he came to see that this was only a part of a much larger problem. Since there was nothing he could do about the marriage—he had ruled out divorce—he decided to tackle the larger problem. As he has achieved a degree of financial security, he was in a position to explore a large number of hobbies as well as a career change. So from this time on, Donald's therapy became a process of exploring and playing with various interests and career options rather than marital problems.

Gradually, after considering all kinds of ideas and changes, this process led Donald to leave his business and get into politics—something he always had a passion for. He was eventually elected to his town's council and focused his attention on local welfare and health care issues. He was then happy not only because he loved his new work but, even more critically, because he felt so good about his ability to make the change. For the first time in his life he felt free—free from his own drive and free from the fear of instability. Not unpredictably, this sense of freedom relieved him almost completely from his critical, judgmental feelings toward his wife. In turn, feeling more accepted by her husband, Elena responded with a greater sense of self-confidence, assertiveness, and independence—which was what Donald wanted all along.

6

Sexual Love

Do Majesty and love go well together
Or linger in one dwelling? Hardly
OVID

Jupiter, the ruler of all gods, often took advantage of his powers in order to pursue sexual companionships with women. When he desired Europa, the daughter of the king of Tyre, he took on the form of a bull, and after an elaborate and playful seduction he literally swept the unsuspecting girl off her feet. Then, with the girl on his back, he galloped across the ocean to a new land, which he promptly named after her. There, resuming his normal form and explaining his reasons for kidnapping her, he won her consent for their sexual union. And after they had sex, Jupiter returned to the safety of his home and wife, leaving Europa to fend for herself in the new land.

This is a story about raw, powerful, and uninhibited male sexuality, symbolized, of course, by the ungodly bull. The woman, it should be noted, is not nearly as passive as it initially appears, and we'll come back to the role of female sexuality vis-à-vis Sexual Love in a moment. For now, what's interesting to me about this myth is that the omnipotent god, Jupiter, who could have had Europa in any number of ways, needed to shed his majesty and become the quintessential male animal in order to conquer her. To appreciate the relevance of this transformation, we needn't look further than some of our present-day cultural icons, for example, the U.S. president who temporarily shed the apparent character of presidential demeanor, superior intellect, and concern for people in order to pursue a young intern and engage her in what appeared to be a strictly sexual dialogue.

Now while we may find it easy to judge such behavior in others, if we try hard enough, we may also find it in ourselves. The fact of the matter is that this kind of sexual split—whether we act on it or not—is something we all share. If we are not Bill Clinton, who acted out, then we are Jimmy Carter, who sinned in his heart, and while there are psychological and practical differences between sexual action and sexual fantasy, both can be equally compelling as well as compulsive. And both can create an intoxicating illusion of love.

STEP ONE: RECOGNIZING YOUR PATTERN

Aaron came to see me after his wife of two years tore up his clothes and threw him out of the house when she found evidence that he had had sex with another woman in their home. Aaron admitted he had done it, saying he had been in love with this woman for several months now, tried to resist it all this time, but finally gave in. He explained that while he cared for and respected his wife, Anne, he felt that the other woman, Judy, was his true soul mate. Whereas Anne was "squeaky clean"—a loyal friend, a good housewife, and a great future mother—Judy was more like him, a "downtown type." A black leather girl and a sexy dancer, she was also more philosophical about life.

And for some time after he separated from Anne it appeared as though he and Judy were developing a very special, deep relationship. They were completely open and honest with each other, spending days together talking, taking trips, and having the most wonderful sex. I was a little suspicious when Aaron described their lovemaking as an ongoing series of hours-long, multiple-orgasm sessions, culminating every time in a blissful state of total merger and total exhaustion, which furthermore totally matched his favorite sexual fantasy of entering a woman with his head and swimming into her insides. But at first, I analyzed my suspiciousness away as a mere indication of my own envy . . .

My suspicion, however, quickly returned when Aaron told me about some of his past sexual experiences. For example, he once had sex with a woman in the elevator of the Empire State Building, stopping and starting between floors, and another time only a few feet away from the actual drop of the Grand Canyon. In addition, as we were discussing this, Aaron's relationship with his "soul mate," Judy, was already beginning to deteriorate. Eventually, after a series of fights, accusations, and misunderstandings, Judy decided to get back together with her husband, whom she had left a few months before meeting Aaron. Aaron was devastated by the breakup but also relieved, and in a short time he started seeing another woman. After dating her for a few times he started referring to her, self-critically, as his "fuck buddy." They would get together every Tuesday afternoon, have sex, hang out for a bit, and then go their separate ways. After a couple of months of this, Aaron mentioned in therapy that he had not told his "fuck buddy" about his herpes and that it looked like she had just gotten it from him.

Well, by now only a blind (actually deaf) person would fail to recognize the pattern of Sexual Love in Aaron's life. Yes, he "loved women," and yes, he thought he was in love with Judy, but ultimately this love took a primarily sexual form. While we'd covered some of this territory in Aaron's therapy before, I now told him I thought he really had a sexual compulsion, or in popular terms, he was a sex addict. As is often the case with addictions, Aaron first disagreed with my assessment. But after I repeatedly connected the dots for him, he accepted it and agreed to go to a twelve-step group for sexual addictions. After joining the group, he quickly embraced the notion that he was an addict and started building a comprehensive support system for "sober" sexual behavior. And although his group defined sexual sobriety as being sexually active only within a committed relationship, Aaron took it a step further, deciding he would also stop masturbating, which was not something required by the group. This decision, as well as his subsequent daily struggles with painful erections that he could only quell with intensive prayer, all but confirmed the extent of his addiction.

Aaron remained sober, by his definition, for two years, during which time he only kissed a woman he was beginning to date seriously. This courtship failed to take off, but eventually Aaron fell in love with another woman and began a serious and committed relationship, which gradually became fully sexual.

So Aaron's Step One, Recognizing Your Pattern, took about two years to implement! In general terms, this once again demonstrates the regrettable yet undeniable fact that a cognitive or intellectual insight alone is not sufficient to break a behavioral pattern. Ultimately, such insight must be accompanied by an emotional recognition and a process of repetition and practice. More specifically, Aaron's lengthy struggle with Step One sheds light on the power of sexual pleasure to shape human behavior.

When Nancy Reagan embarked on her "Just Say No" antidrug campaign, clinicians and drug addicts alike scoffed at her simple-mindedness. How many times had they heard it before and how little relevance it had to the depth and desperation of addiction! But ironically—while ineffective from a public policy standpoint—saying no to addiction is ultimately the only thing we *can* do. And even though, as in Aaron's case, it involves a process, not an instant, discreet decision, it is nevertheless a decision. It is also noteworthy that unlike drug addiction, sexual compulsions do not involve a physiological dependence on an external substance, and in that respect appear to be easier to overcome. On the other hand, psychologically speaking, they are every bit as addictive. Like drugs, they offer a powerful antidote to depression, loneliness, low self-esteem, and existential emptiness. And clinically speaking, so-called sex addicts often come from families with a history of rampant alcohol and drug abuse and various other compulsions, strongly suggesting a general genetic predisposition.

But having said all that, most people who fall under the spell of Sexual Love are fully able to just say no. If we exclude sexual offenders—who are in a category of their own, combining among other things sexual compulsions with antisocial personality— Aaron's example above, while not uncommon, is probably closer to the extreme end of the continuum between healthy sexual expression and Sexual Love. In other words, there are many people, both men and women, who struggle with the pattern of Sexual Love without being sex addicts. A simple example is that of a female patient who was told by the man she was dating and falling in love with that he was not ready to date her exclusively. She immediately broke up with him and, seeking to escape the pain of rejection, went to a neighborhood bar where she proceeded to flirt with and then kiss another man. When a month later the boyfriend returned and said he was ready to commit, she accepted it and soon thereafter they got engaged. She then told him about kissing that man in the bar. While the fiancé technically had no case against her, this still was a serious threat to the relationship, as the fiancé, as well as the patient herself, were wondering whether it was in her makeup to act out sexually when emotionally pained. This potential crisis in the relationship brought the patient to her Step One. Realizing she was susceptible to it, she resolved to never again follow the path of Sexual Love, a recognition and a resolution that she painfully shared with her fiancé and that helped him to move beyond it.

Now, as contemporary gender roles continue to evolve and to further defy traditional definitions, men's and women's sexual attitudes converge and overlap. Notwithstanding, as I have discussed in *If Men Could Talk*,[2] there is no denying that many, if not most men and women experience their sexuality differently. From an evolutionary standpoint, it's a fact that males, much more so than females, can further their reproductive agenda simply by having more sex. No matter what they do, females cannot have more than one pregnancy at a time. From a cultural perspective, it is quite evident that society expects a certain sexual naughtiness from boys but not from girls. Biologically, there are well-known hormonal as well as genital differences. For example, men usually need a shorter period of time and less direct stimulation to become aroused. This is particularly true at a younger age and with less experience, which is when and how men, or really boys, develop the habits of sexualizing mental contents. In other words, the simplicity of boys' sexual responses—on top of weighty evolutionary, cultural, and hormonal pressures—makes it more likely that they will seek the powerful reward of arousal and orgasm to escape, or cope with, emotional conflict.

Women, on the other hand, are socialized and to some extent "biologized" to explore and express their feelings more directly while at the same time to go along with the male "flow." Certainly this is changing, but when it comes to the exercise of power and leadership, many women still tend to yield, if not subjugate themselves, to men. Of course, the notion of the "woman behind the man"—the Nancy Reagan or Hillary Clinton who

---

[2] Gratch, A., Ph.D. 2002. *If Men Could Talk: Unlocking the Secret Language of Men*. New York: Little, Brown.

actually runs the White House—has some truth to it, suggesting a greater equality than what meets the eye. And similarly, while men often seem to drive the sexual agenda—by initiating it more or by being on top, literally and metaphorically—women often exercise the power of both withholding and initiating. Nevertheless, it is still often the case that women have a hard time saying no. And there's some truth to the paradoxical joke that men talk in order to have sex and women have sex in order to talk. I say "paradoxical," because in a sense, for men sex *is* talking and for women talking *is* sex, or at least sexual, which is to say that it all works out in the end because, ultimately, we are all in it for the same reason—love and intimacy.

But, as you might expect, these gender differences become more polarized and therefore more evident in Sexual Love. It is no coincidence, for example, that Aaron's twelve-step group for sexual addiction consisted entirely of men. At the same time, these men were sex addicts, not masturbation addicts, meaning, they had partners and, most of the time, partners who themselves were not sex addicts but rather love addicts (which in a way we all are). In other words, many women who fall prey to the pattern of Sexual Love present a different clinical picture than their male partners. For one thing, women are often in denial about the fact that their date or boyfriend is (consciously or unconsciously) basically only interested in sex. They either believe the man who says, or they tell themselves, "This can become a relationship." My own clinical experience suggests that, sometimes, even women who consciously engage in a "fling," or a casual sexual relationship, in retrospect end up feeling that they have been used. Men, on the other hand, often end up feeling guilty that they have used the woman, even though she was clearly a free agent. There is no justice or perhaps even logic to it, yet this is often the case.

These gender differences clearly have repercussions for

achieving Step One. The bottom line is that in order to say no to Sexual Love both men and women need to be able to read the signs of Sexual Love. While both genders need to learn to recognize signs of sexual compulsivity and of the complementary "love addiction" and denial, women are more likely to need to recognize the former in their partners and the latter in themselves. And the reverse is true for men.

In reading the red flags below, you will quickly know which to apply to yourself and which to others. For convenience sake, however, I'm directing the diagnostic signs to the female reader who is more likely to assume the traditional female role in Sexual Love. Of course, there are many exceptions to this, both male and female, and if you are one of them, please forgive my political incorrectness and simply adjust the direction of the red flags to your situation.

Reading the Tea Leaves for Sexual Compulsiveness

- Your boyfriend is not interested in being with you in times and places where sex cannot occur. Often this means he doesn't want to meet your family and friends and doesn't enjoy simply hanging out with you for brunch, in the park, or in a coffee shop.
- The man you are dating is a slick, smooth talker. He oozes warmth and compliments. His lines seem too perfect, showing no signs of nervousness or insecurity. He makes his move too fast, giving the impression of a talented, serial seducer.
- You feel you are being pressured or manipulated to have sex. Rather than telling you, "I really want it but I'll wait as long as it takes," the guy you are dating seems to be saying, "I want it now or I'm out of here."
- Your boyfriend is often evasive about his whereabouts and

you catch him in a lie. This may mean other, nonsexual secrets, but see if you can connect the dots with additional data (e.g., your gynecologist informs you that you have vaginal warts or herpes, and you haven't had sex with anyone else in the past couple of years).

- After having unprotected sex with you for a while, the man you are dating confesses he has herpes.

- You respond to a Match.com profile and e-mail back and forth. You give him your phone number and he calls. You talk for a while and he then seduces you into having phone sex.

- Your boyfriend or husband "adores" you, especially in bed, idealizing your body and beauty, but you feel he is not interested in who you are.

- Your boyfriend or husband insists on having sex in only one way or position, which makes you uncomfortable. For example, he *has* to go through an elaborate role-play, pretending you are his secretary in order to ejaculate. Or he insists on enlivening your sex life by inviting a third person to join. This is different from the *two of you wanting to experiment* with joint fantasy, role-play, or even a third party.

- You find out the man you are dating has videotaped the two of you during sex.

- Your boyfriend or husband is not interested in sex with you. This can be a sign he has a secret sex life (in reality or fantasy).

- Your boyfriend or husband is only interested in pleasing you. He doesn't have an erection and doesn't want to be stimulated by you (same as above).

- The man you are dating tells you he frequently goes to nude bars and gets lap dances. You tell him this bothers you, but he thinks that's your problem.

- The man you are dating tells you he cheated on some girlfriends before. This without indication of genuine regret and without insight into the seriousness of the problem. For example, he might say, "Yeah, I did cheat on a couple of girls which I guess wasn't right, but they weren't exactly God's gift to the earth either."
- The man you are dating mentions, perhaps in passing, that he is a sex addict—this without an indication that he has been through an ongoing recovery program. (This may seem obvious, but then again, in their search for love, love junkies often deny the obvious.)

Well, as you can see, the list can go on and on . . . but I think you get the picture.

Reading the Tea Leaves for Love Addiction and Denial

- You meet a charming man in a bar and he invites you to go back to his place. You don't really feel like it—you're tired and you have a job interview the next day—but he is persistent and persuasive so you end up doing it anyway, rationalizing that you really need to meet men if you're ever going to get married.
- You hear from a friend of a friend that the cool guy you just started dating is a "player." A coworker of yours who also happens to know him says he's a real drinker and that he once approached him for a two-thousand-dollar loan, even though they were only casual acquaintances. The guy himself tells you he recently broke up with a girl because she wanted a commitment and he wasn't ready for it. You tell yourself, "I shouldn't dismiss someone because of rumors, and you never know how the relationship will

develop—maybe the last girlfriend was just not the right person for him."

- You meet someone on Match.com and after a few e-mails he gives you his phone number. You call and have a great conversation and you feel this has real potential. Then, toward the end of the conversation, he mentions he is "a little bit into rough sex." This doesn't feel right but you tell yourself, "He is so open and communicative" or "He probably just wants to experiment with being more masculine or assertive—and why not? I like strong men."

- After a couple of brief relationships in which the man broke up with you after having sex a couple of times, you vow to take it more slowly in the next relationship. But now you find yourself on a second date with a man who says all the right things—including "I don't take sex lightly"—and you end up making love to him.

- While talking about sex or pornography, the man you are dating mentions in passing, "I am probably a sex addict myself," but while you first think it's a weird comment, you quickly dismiss it as a joke or you forget about it and don't bring it up again.

- Your boyfriend asks you to engage in sexual practices that you think are off the wall and you don't feel comfortable with, but you go along anyway, rationalizing that you are doing something special for him.

- Your boyfriend and you have wonderful, passionate sex and deep philosophical conversations about life. But he doesn't want to meet your friends and says he is not ready for a commitment. He also tells you he spends a couple of hours a day watching pornography online. You talk about it to your best friend—who used to work with your boyfriend—and she reminds you that she had warned you when you first met him that he wasn't relationship material. You now remember that at the time you thought she was just jealous. You're beginning to worry she may have been right, but you decide to give the relationship more time.

- You have a fight with your boyfriend and you don't talk to each other for a couple of days. He then calls to apologize and you make up. You later hear from a friend that in one of those nights after the fight he was dancing with another girl in a downtown club. You ask him about it. He is evasive and vague but eventually confesses he had slept with this girl. He is now tearful and remorseful and asks for your forgiveness. You feel bad for him and you tell yourself, "I guess that's what guys are like."

This list can also be interminable, but it's all really a variation on the same theme, which is, if you find yourself rationalizing and explaining and analyzing your date's or boyfriend's or husband's sexual behavior as a means of accepting and colluding with it, you should know it's time to just say no. Saying no, of course, is not merely disagreeing or arguing or fighting—these in themselves can work in the service of denial. For example, every month when paying the phone bill, a female patient was confronted with close to one hundred dollars of phone calls to a certain number, which, when she finally checked it out, turned out to be a phone sex establishment. She confronted her husband about it and he told her he was doing research for a new business idea. "I don't believe you," she yelled. "How can you lie to me like this? You think I'm some kind of a moron?" A big fight ensued and the patient didn't talk to her husband for a few days. Gradually, they warmed up to each other again and the incident was forgotten. The phone calls stopped for a couple of months but then reappeared with increased frequency. The moral: just saying no is about actions, not words.

STEP TWO: UNDERSTANDING YOUR AMBIVALENCE

Freud saw sexual symbolism everywhere, but in contrast to this tendency he famously observed that "sometimes a cigar is just a cigar." To paraphrase Freud, it can also be said that sometimes a penis is just a cigar, which is to say that sex is not about sex after all but rather about our psyche or soul. And while men tend to sexualize emotional conflicts more so than women do, both genders use the sexual arena to deal with nonsexual issues. This means that if we want to say good-bye to relationships where love equals sex and hello to relationships where love is greater than sex, we must first desexualize our emotional conflicts.

A couple in their late twenties came to see me because of a "sexual problem" that threatened their otherwise rich and committed relationship. As the girlfriend saw the problem, the boyfriend wasn't interested in having sex with her and often avoided it with all kinds of excuses. The boyfriend—who was an extremely likable man and who by the girlfriend's own words was the most loving and considerate man she had ever known— admitted as much but said he didn't know what the problem was. But after we decided that he and I would try to get to the bottom of it in individual therapy, he confided in me that he actually did know what the problem was. It turned out that this genuinely sweet man was only able to get aroused by fantasizing about raping and shooting women. While he felt horrible about these fantasies, he had never acted on them in any way, knowing full well that they were only fantasies. But whereas he came to terms with having to "use" these fantasies while masturbating, he didn't want to use them in such a way while making love with the girlfriend he loved so much. So he basically avoided sex with her as much as possible.

While this patient presented with a sexual problem that impaired his sex life, his therapy eventually revealed that the problem was emotional and interpersonal rather than sexual. In brief, as a child the patient was physically abused and humiliated by his mother. So, growing up fearful of her, he withdrew into violent revenge fantasies, which at puberty attached themselves to the sexual impulse directed at all women. It was as if in his sexual fantasies he were reversing the balance of power in his relationship with his mother—this time he was the one in control, venting his rage (psychiatrist Robert Stollar has described this process as "turning trauma into triumph"). It was, of course, no coincidence that the patient was consciously and behaviorally extremely thoughtful and loving. As a child, he was too scared of his rage, so he had expelled all traces of hostility and aggression from his conscious interaction with people. Another way of putting it is that, based on his experience with his mother, the patient was angry with women but could experience it only through the emotionally dissociated channel of sexual fantasies.

So for this patient, therapy consisted of "desexualizing" his fantasies, that is, helping him to get in touch with his anger toward women and ultimately toward his mother. This, in turn, would make him less of a pleasant, loving person, because now he would be more easily bothered and angered by his girlfriend or mother. On the other hand, he would no longer need to rely on violent fantasies to express his anger and, as a result, might be able to have a better sex life. In other words, while previously there wasn't even a hint of ambivalence in his love—except, of course, in his inexplicable avoidance of sex—now the ambivalence would be more in the open. In truth, it would take time and work along the lines of Step Three, Resolving Your Ambivalence, to completely neutralize the violent fantasies. But recognizing that these fantasies are *relational* rather than *sexual* is at the heart of Step Two, Understanding Your Ambivalence.

While this example is perhaps extreme, less violent versions of its basic premise—that through displacement, sex or sexual fantasies are used to express unacceptable aggressive feelings we might have for our love object—are quite common. Certainly in many long-term relationships, but even in many dating situations, one or both partners frequently develop a version of what Freud called the Madonna/Whore complex. This is a sexual way of managing ambivalence: you love and respect your primary partner, but you have sexual fantasies (or an actual sexual relationship) with another, less-respected partner. You "make love" with the former and "fuck" the latter. You have foreplay and intercourse with one and oral sex or anal sex or other forms of sex that you might feel are more exciting to you yet degrading to your partner with the other. In this way you protect the purity of your primary relationship from your aggression. More accurately, you *pretend* you protect it, while in reality, your ambivalence is expressed sexually: you are less aroused or not at all aroused by your primary partner, you channel your sexual energy elsewhere, and you might even need to have so-called replacement fantasies in order to sexually perform with your partner.

Many people wonder if it's "okay" (normal, healthy, etc.) to have sex with their partner while fantasizing about someone else. To me it's not a question of right or wrong but rather of how you express your ambivalence—in this case, sexually. If, as is often the case, you don't tell your partner about such replacement fantasies, it's probably because you feel guilty, which suggests it's not okay with *you*. From a psychological standpoint, it's not that you are doing something wrong; it's that you are not willing to own your ambivalence. You unconsciously hide it inside your sexual functioning, only to end up feeling there's something wrong with you or your partner *sexually*.

So in Step Two your job is to translate uncomfortable or hidden sexual desires and preferences—yours and/or your partner's—into emotional, interpersonal communications. While in some cases this requires the help of an experienced therapist, often enough you can do it on your own. For example, many women have sexual fantasies about a powerful man raping or, short of that, somehow taking control of their bodies and forcing them to have sex. You can easily analyze this type of fantasy in isolation, reading it as an indication that you want a strong man to take charge of your nonsexual interactions or perhaps even to protect you. But to make it even more useful, you can try to relate this wish in some meaningful way to the reality of your life. Clinical experience shows that this type of fantasy often occurs in women who have an aggressive, take-charge interpersonal style and who therefore have a hard time giving up control in intimate relationships. They date or marry kind, sensitive, or passive men so that they can be in charge but then wish that their partner would be stronger or more aggressive so that they can relax or feel protected by him. This wish, however, is inconsistent with their partner's personality, as well as with their own need to be in control. So they end up expressing it through a sexual fantasy or role-play.

Sexual fantasies and role-plays can be very arousing but are often emotionally flat or dissociated. When you are aroused by fantasizing about being tied up or raped, you don't *feel* helpless or victimized. After all, the whole scenario is your creation and you've created it for your own thrill. In other words, the "negative" feelings are expressed in the content of your fantasy but are still not experienced by you consciously. As we have seen, however, in addition to the content itself, there are sometimes feelings of guilt over the fantasy, which are also indicative of "bad" or negative feelings toward the other person.

While perhaps some of the most common, aggression and dominance (or their opposites, as described above) are hardly the only problematic sentiments to be expressed sexually. All difficult feelings make their way into the bedroom. One young man, who was a successful money manager on Wall Street, fell in love with a struggling artist who by all accounts was smart, beautiful, and sexy. However, she was highly demanding of him in many respects. First, she would often call him to come help her with one thing or another in the middle of the workday. Second, because she had no money and no health insurance, she gradually came to rely on him for various financial needs and crises. Finally, she had high and very particular sexual expectations, insisting, for example, that they look into each other's eyes intently during lovemaking, for the entire duration. The patient loved her and serviced her without much complaining, in part because it actually turned him on. Ironically, it all became a problem when she once demanded to know what he was thinking about during intercourse. Complying as usual, he answered he was fantasizing that she was a vampire sucking on his neck and emptying him out. Upon hearing that, the girlfriend jumped out of bed horrified, saying "So that's what you think about me, that I'm sucking the life out of you . . . that I'm using you . . . You don't know anything about love . . ."

This was the beginning of the end of their relationship, as my patient understood that the girlfriend's interpretation of his sexual fantasy was in fact correct: he was so drawn to her that he had denied to himself the feeling that he was being sucked dry by this woman. But the girlfriend's "translation" of his sexual fantasy snapped him into recognition, and from that time on he tried to get some of his own needs met in the relationship. But while he was now struggling to acknowledge and deal with this ambivalence, the girlfriend wouldn't yield on her demands (including her "demand" that he should not have such sexual fantasies) and she soon broke up with him. Subsequently, the patient realized that his attraction to this woman was all but a manifestation of Sexual Love. The girlfriend was even correct in saying he didn't know much about love—which is not to say that she did.

Interestingly, this patient, who was basically heterosexual, had another "sucking" fantasy, in which he would have oral sex with men, sucking out all their sperm. When we explored this more, it turned out that in the fantasy he believed that he needed this external "resupply" of sperm in order to continue to function sexually with women. Now if you put this in nonsexual terms you might say that feeling depleted by women, the patient needed some support from men, which upon further exploration defined quite precisely his childhood experience with his parents. His mother was needy and overprotective, always giving him the feeling that she was "taking" rather than "giving," even when, for example, giving him a hug. He thus longed to get away from her smothering presence and looked to his father for strength and support. But the father was passive and withdrawn and away on business for much of the time. So to oversimplify, his sexual fantasies came down to having too much of mother and too little of father. How unusual . . .

To summarize, if you want to understand your own or your partner's sexual interests, which is a must if you want to overcome Sexual Love, try to see if they relate to nonsexual conflicts in your life. If you are attracted to younger, boyish men, ask yourself if you are afraid of being in a more equal relationship. Check to see if you are surrounded by "yes men" and if you have a reason to be fearful of "real" men; ask yourself if your father or older brother was a bully and if you therefore generalize this perception to all men, except for those young, sweet-looking ones. You might be afraid of men or even "hate" men but can only express such feelings by being sexually drawn to "nonmen."

Similarly, if you are unable to reach orgasm, ask yourself if you are open to receiving and experiencing pleasure in other ways. Do you value being self-sufficient to such an extent that you cannot let someone in? Do you always have to be in control, because to be vulnerable would mean to be taken advantage of? Can you only let go when drinking? Do you experience emotionally giving people as intrusive? Do you feel that to receive is to be forced? Did you grow up with an intrusive parent, or do you feel your boyfriend or husband is intrusive or dominating?

If your boyfriend or husband has been struggling with impotence, try to figure out if he feels inadequate in other areas of his life: Has he suffered a setback in his career? Does he feel emasculated by you in some way? Of course, impotence can mean many things (he might be paralyzed by performance anxiety, he might be having an affair and feeling guilty about it, he might be gay, etc.). But with the exception of physically based erectile dysfunction, impotence *always* represents some kind of ambivalence, some wish on his part to not be there or not to perform. Which is why women often interpret impotence as something that somehow reflects on them, as in "I'm not attractive enough" or "I must be doing something wrong." But it has *nothing* to do with you: it's all about how he manages his ambivalence, in this case, by expressing it sexually. At the same time, since it always takes two to tango, you might inadvertently or unconsciously play a role in this script. For instance, if he is not doing as well as you at work these days and you are losing respect for him, or if you are somehow judgmental and intimidating, he might well be communicating his feelings about this by withdrawing sexually. Of course, consciously, his sexual "communication" in this case only reinforces his sense of inadequacy. But unconsciously he feels liberated via his perception that at last he is not complying with your expectations.

Finally, if your boyfriend always seems to be checking out younger girls, ask yourself if there are other ways in which he is refusing to grow up. Does he live in a messy bachelor apartment, smoke pot, and go out to rock concerts much of the time? Is he working only part time and not thinking about his future? Does he avoid taking adult actions or tend to live in a fantasy world? There is nothing you can do about his sexual interest in younger women, but if you determine that this in fact is not a sexual problem, you are in a better position to help him "grow up," which eventually may impact on his sexual interests as well.

This last point is probably true for all of the above scenarios, which is to say that in and of itself understanding the nonsexual meaning of sexual behavior doesn't automatically change this behavior. Indeed, the purpose of understanding this behavior is not to change it but rather to accept it. Understanding that it's an expression of his ambivalence, you can accept your partner's impotence (or whatever sexual symptom) and try to help him with that nonsexual ambivalence. Alternatively, understanding it's an expression of your own ambivalence, you accept your attraction to boyish men (or whatever sexual symptom) and you try to work on this nonsexual ambivalence. If you can't accept these sexual behaviors, you are back to Step One and you break off the relationship. But if you do accept them, you are ready to move on to Step Three, where, naturally, your work is still cut out for you.

STEP THREE: RESOLVING YOUR AMBIVALENCE

Resolving sexually expressed ambivalence is difficult but not impossible. It's difficult because our sexual interests and tastes have been repeatedly reinforced with the powerful motivators or be-havioral rewards of sexual arousal, climax, and release. Whatever the original developmental causes of our sexual tastes—the kind of repressed ambivalence discussed here or even genetic and biological determinants that surely play a role—the easy accessi-bility and basic physicality of the reward, especially in masturba-tory fantasies, continuously reinforce them. For that reason, when trying to resolve Sexual Love, we should focus not on re-jecting our existing proclivities but rather on expanding our repertoire. Take the not uncommon case of the man who can only get aroused or ejaculate when receiving oral sex. His Step Two awareness that he needs a woman to "service" him because he is ambivalent about equality in intimacy, should bring him in Step Three not to attempt to eradicate his love for oral sex but rather to expand his interests to sexual activities that represent greater equality in intimacy.

Generally speaking, most forms of Sexual Love involve some kind of a repetitive, inflexible sexual behavior. We become so fix-ated on one thing—conquest, oral sex, new sex, youth, mastur-bation, wanting to be tied up, fear of penetration, wanting to please the other, you name it—that our sexual habits become rigid and limited. We thus fail to integrate other sexual activities and the kind of intimacy they represent into our relationship. So, as in the other patterns of failed love, in Step Three too our goal is integration. What we strive to accomplish is not only to accept the ambivalence but also to bring together into relative harmony our warring, conflicted feelings about love and the people we love. In the case of Sexual Love, this means, first and foremost, *overcoming the dynamic of sexual opposites.* Let me explain.

One of my patients was a beautiful, married woman in her late thirties who came to see me because she fell in love and started an affair with the minister of her church. In taking her history, I found out that between the ages of nine and eleven she had a sexual relationship with a brother who was four years older. He never physically forced her, but he certainly initiated it. Furthermore, he cajoled and pressured her to the point where she felt unable to say no, and so she went along with it even though she knew it was wrong. Later, as an older teenager, she dated many boys and rather quickly became sexually active and promiscuous. As a young woman she often found herself seeking approval and love from men who were in it for the sex and who would usually lose interest after a couple of times.

Her husband, however, was a different story, which was why she married him. A junior high school English teacher, he was more gentle and soft-spoken, and less sex-driven than those other men. And he truly loved her. She was somewhat less attracted to him, but she loved him too and they had a good relationship. But now, several years into their marriage and as a mother of two young girls, she couldn't help falling in love with the minister of their church, who was older, much loved, and highly respected in their community.

When she started sleeping with him, she became overwhelmed with feelings of love and spirituality. After a few months of therapy, she confessed to her husband and then left home to be with the minister. But because of her lover's position in the church, the relationship had to be kept a secret, and after a few months it became clear to both me and the patient that under the guise of spiritual love, she and the minister had engaged largely in a physical—sensual, erotic, and carnal—relationship. There was nothing wrong with these sexual feelings and experiences, except that now the old feelings of being used by a man began to creep in. As the patient herself put it at one point, "I thought I was making love to God, but really I am just fucking a gigolo."

This, for the patient was Step One: she broke up the relationship and moved back in with her husband, who, lovingly, was willing to forgive her if she committed to work on her issues.

She did that in therapy with me and in time reached Step Two, seeing that like her premarital experiences with men, her relationship with the minister was a reenactment of the incestuous relationship with her brother. Secretly and shamefully she went along with something she felt was wrong, trying to get love and approval from a man who ultimately just wanted to use her sexually. Why the reenactment? Simply put, over the years she learned to love and desire what initially had been imposed on her, so that she could repeat in the active what she had suffered from more passively as a child. If you repeat the same scenario again and again—so goes the logic of the unconscious— eventually you'll come out on top and get the love you need. Realizing all this, the patient also came to recognize her ambivalence toward men: in her eyes, her husband was nice but not so attractive or sexually exciting, and the minister was attractive and exciting but a user and a taker. Of course, these qualities may have objectively resided in these men, but to the extent that they did they "fit" quite nicely into her preexisting ambivalent perception of men.

Now that the patient was back with her husband, she started the hard work of Step Three. Here, she had to compare her sexual relationship with her husband with her sexual relationships with the minister and the other men earlier in her life. The comparison immediately yielded two opposites. With her husband it was sweet, affectionate, and cuddly, sometimes just a foreplay without climaxing, as he occasionally had erection difficulties and she wasn't always aroused; with the others it was supercharged, obsessive, and rough, often culminating in multiple orgasms and physical pain. With her husband it was safe and comfortable; with the others risky and shameful. Clearly, this split related to her history of sexual abuse: on the one hand she had to repeat the trauma of a sexualized relationship with an older brother in order to overcome it, but on the other, she would turn to the safety of a nonsexual or less sexual, loving, and benign father figure. The truth, of course, was that the minister and those other men were not her brother and that her husband was not her father. Both were distortions in which she played the role of the helpless little girl, also a distortion. So her job in Step Three was to integrate this split within her primary relationship. That is, she had to work on preserving the sweet and loving nature of her marital sex while adding to it some of the hard-core aspects of the other sex.

To accomplish that, the patient had to insist that she needed *both* of these opposites in her life. She already knew that she couldn't give up on her husband, but now I told her that she couldn't quite give up on the "minister" either—or at least on the kind of passion he represented. What she needed was to find the golden, middle path in the relationship to which she was committed, her marriage. This was not easy as she began to realize that she didn't feel comfortable being merely a sex object with her husband—that belonged in the minister's bed. But then she and her husband began to experiment. At first it didn't go well, because over the years her husband was conditioned by her—and of course by his own corresponding dynamic that discouraged him from being sexually aggressive with women—to not view her as a sex object. So when she became more overtly sexual or "graphic," he would panic and lose his erection. But then one day, after several attempts, he rose to the occasion and got into it. Then gradually, by trial and error and with more experimentation and practice, they got closer and closer to integrating these opposites—of "lovemaking" and "fucking"—into their sex life. And eventually they ended up somewhere in the middle.

This splitting of our sexuality into polar opposites is often a result of sexual abuse or of inappropriate sexual stimulation in childhood. The patient above reacted to the sexual abuse she had suffered by becoming overly sexual. Other victims of early sexual abuse react by avoiding sex altogether. But as is always the case with polar opposites, these two reactions are yin-yang complements that contain, and therefore can be transformed into, each other. The woman who reacts by having a lot of sex is trying to repeat the experience in order to feel differently about it so as to undo the past, and the one who avoids sex altogether does so also to undo the past. The former might eventually conclude that sex is indeed a bad thing and reject it, thus turning into the latter, while the latter might eventually feel she misses sex so much that she will turn into the former. But of course neither extreme is good—it's all about integration.

This dynamic of sexual opposites points to an important paradox regarding the pattern of Sexual Love: in many cases the absence of sex from one's life is part and parcel of the pattern of Sexual Love. We've seen before the case of a man who avoided sex with his partner because his sexual fantasies were too disturbing to him and the case of the sexual addict who went into complete abstinence. It is also likely that many men who go into professions that require sexual abstinence do so because they are afraid of their own rather intense sexuality. This, in my mind, explains many of the cases of sexual abuse in the Catholic Church.

But this dynamic is not limited to the province of sexual abuse and trauma. It pervades our daily sexual lives in obvious, as well as more subtle ways. I've touched before on that most common of male afflictions, impotence, where again, the absence of sex appears to be a sexual problem. Let's now visit a related and also frequent male malady, this time by way of illustrating how to apply Step Three to Sexual Love.

George was a single internist in his late thirties. He was "at last" dating a woman he was serious about, and they were talking about engagement and marriage. This brought him to my office because he wanted to tackle a sexual problem that had bothered him for a long time. "You may have guessed," he said. "I'm talking about erectile dysfunction, which I've had on and off since adolescence. It didn't bother me so much before because my relationships were never serious enough and also because I was able to compensate for it."

"I'm still able to compensate," he went on, "but I now want to deal with it. Years ago, I saw an urologist who diagnosed a diminished blood flow to the penis and suggested penile injections to stimulate an erection. I couldn't deal with that, but in the past couple of years I've used Viagra. It certainly helps, but I still need my fantasies to ejaculate." Perhaps because he was a physician, as he spoke I was thinking about the doctor's rule of thumb that you listen to the symptoms, not the patient. In the psychologist's office, however, the patient *is* the symptoms, so in listening to him I couldn't help noticing that his self-diagnosis of impotence was inconsistent with what he said about being able to compensate and needing his fantasies. So I asked him what he meant by these words.

As it turned out, George's impotence was intermittent and situational. He was able to get an erection when masturbating or being masturbated but would sometimes lose it after penetrating his partner. Similarly, he was able to ejaculate with certain fantasies but not with others, and it was more difficult during intercourse. This, of course, showed that the problem was not physiological but rather psychological. In addition, it was technically not impotence but rather a partial and situational inhibited male orgasm. I say "partial" because he could come at times and "situational" because it depended on the situation, in this case, the nature of his fantasies.

George, it should be noted, had completed Step One on his own, before setting foot in my office: he had committed to his girlfriend despite his sexual problem, effectively saying no to his previously interminable search for the perfect sexual stimulus. He was therefore ready to immediately engage in the work of Step Two by exploring the nonsexual aspect of his difficulties. This proved to be relatively easy as the fantasies that aroused him and that he used successfully in masturbation (or as replacement fantasies that enabled him to ejaculate during intercourse) were clearly a variation on a theme. In one fantasy he would imagine having sex with his housekeeper, in another with a toothless, whorish woman, and in a third with a young nurse in his medical practice. All these fantasies featured oral or anal sex along with the use of dildos, fists, and explicit language. The theme, in other words, was that of hard-core sex with women whom he saw as less than his equal.

By contrast, with the women he had dated, and especially with his current girlfriend, sex was about gentle and considerate lovemaking with someone who was not only his equal but whom he perceived as his superior. His current girlfriend, for one thing, was an accomplished political columnist and he was intellectually intimidated by her. In other words, his sexuality consisted of two polar opposites, one involving gentle love, the other aggressive objectification. The former he practiced with the woman he loved, the latter with women he lusted for. But realizing that lust doesn't last, George relegated the latter strictly to fantasy. The problem with that approach—and as we've seen, this Madonna/Whore complex is quite common—is that these opposites continuously and reciprocally reinforce each other's assumed incompatibility, a dynamic that guarantees a boring or a dysfunctional sex life in one's primary relationship. Clearly, what George wanted was to have it both ways but integrated into his relationships rather than split. However, because he was afraid that his objectification of women would interfere with his love for them, he had created that split, objectifying only women he did not respect.

Now, as we discussed this in therapy, George came to see that these opposites were not, in fact, enemies. And he agreed that he should embrace both so that he could treat his girlfriend both with respect and as a sex object. But while he understood this intellectually, it was difficult for him to practice it in bed—first, because as I've said, changing sexual tastes is quite difficult and, second, because he was intimidated by his girlfriend and didn't know how to broach it with her.

This is where Step Three came into the picture. Not only did George fail to bring his aggression into the bedroom, he also didn't really bring it to the living room. So that's where we started, helping him to confront the girlfriend when she would relate to him in a condescending manner, sneering that he was not on top of current affairs or not all that verbally articulate. George began to disagree with her, rejecting her criticism of his thoughts and intellect. Initially, the girlfriend was taken aback and they were both unhappy about the fights that ensued. But with time she actually grew to respect him more and was consequently less critical of him. And he, in turn, felt reassured that she could evidently tolerate his newly found aggression.

So feeling more confident and firm, George now decided to share some of his sexual fantasies with his girlfriend and to express his desire to integrate them into the relationship. The girlfriend was first upset—for her own reasons, she too was afraid of male aggression and was fine with coasting with unexciting but gentle lovemaking. But she was open to some experimentation, which eventually resulted in greater arousal and less inhibition on George's part. Their sex life thus followed the same trajectory of their overall relationship: from the denial of ambivalence, to expressing it through conflict, to greater and greater integration.

In truly long-term relationships and marriages, the couple's sex life comes under such constant pressures as familiarity, tiredness, the unattractiveness of daily intimacies, work-related stress, and the presence of children. But the internal psychological conflict of sexual opposites poses an even greater challenge. While a full integration and the "best" possible sex in a thirty-year marriage is probably the exception rather than the rule, striving for it is better than giving up. Indeed, resolving sexually expressed ambivalence is a work in progress. Yet the idea of integration is not a fantasy. It is based, to a large extent, on one of Freud's more profound observations, which is that behind every fear there is a wish. So if you are afraid of bringing aggression into your sexuality, it's because you want to and you are afraid of your own wish. Acknowledging this can go a long way toward developing a sex life that accommodates both the fear and the wish.

In practical terms this means you can improve your sex life by becoming a little bit of your own opposite: if you tend to be the passive partner, try to initiate sex more; if you are sexually more needy than your partner, experiment with holding back; if you only like "lovemaking," experiment with "fucking"—and vice versa. Of course, as we saw, we might have to tackle this first in the nonsexual arena. This brings us to the last of the failed love patterns, where, as we shall see, this dynamic of opposites is an ever-present—and mostly nonsexual—challenge.

7

Androgynous Love

*So these two joined in close embrace, no longer
Two beings, and no longer man and woman,
But neither, and yet both.*
OVID

You are about to hear the story of a fountain, Salmacis, with an evil reputation, Because its waters make men weak and feeble . . ." This is how Ovid starts the story of Hermaphroditus and Salmacis. Hermaphroditus was a handsome youth who was so named because he resembled both his father, Hermes, and his mother, Aphrodite. Salmacis was a lustful water nymph. Basically, the story is about how Salmacis lures Hermaphroditus into her pool and then tries to jump his bones. Wrapping herself around him like a serpent she prays to the gods, "May no day ever come to separate us!" Her prayer is then heard and their two bodies merge together, with one head and one body, both a woman and a man.

Amazingly, when it comes to relationships between men and women, this ancient story is more relevant today than ever before. In the wake of the women's movement, when women are encouraged to pursue interests previously thought of as in the male domain, and men are expected to be sensitive and vulnerable in the more feminine tradition, we are all hermaphrodites. Prior to the women's movement, the war between the sexes was fought along rigidly defined sex roles. When a marriage or a relationship was in crisis, it was often because the couple was polarized along the stereotypical feminine-masculine fault line. The man was logical and unfeeling and was only interested in action movies, sex, cars, and sports. And the woman was emotional and sensitive with an interest in romantic comedies, the opera, books, and gossip. In the therapist's office, these couples tried to avoid their ambivalence about each other's gender by arguing that the other person must change their gender-based behavior. "Be more sensitive so that I don't have to accept that men are clueless," the woman would say. "Be less emotional so that I don't have to accept that women are hysterical," would say the man.

Of course, such couples still abound, but nowadays marital therapists see more and more couples who are polarized along the same masculine-feminine dimension, but in reverse. In the hermaphrodite couple—which theoretically should be ideal as each partner can have the best of both worlds—the man is sensitive and open while the woman is strong and assertive. In this relationship, the man falls in love with a woman he perceives as a tough, independent person whom he can respect, and the woman falls in love with a man she perceives as an emotionally supportive person with whom she can connect. If this couple ends up in the therapist's office, it's because they weren't careful about what they had wished for. "Tell her she needs to be more feminine," the man now begs the therapist. "Tell him to be a man," barks the woman.

When couples are polarized along gender roles, whether in the traditional or the more contemporary, reversed form, their only hope is to find the middle ground. This depends, first and foremost, on their ability to accept their ambivalent feelings about their partner's gender. But let's not put the cart before the horse: this polarization is a problem not only for couples, but also, and perhaps even more so, for singles. In my experience, the inability of many single men and women to accept their ambivalence about the other gender is one of the most important reasons they have difficulties meeting the right person. This is often not talked about for fear of being politically incorrect. Many professional single women complain that men cannot handle their success. "Men want to be with a woman who is less successful or less intelligent—basically submissive," they tell their therapist, "so I'm screwed." The therapist, agreeing that women should be free to pursue an aggressive career, can find himself agreeing with the patient. But there is a difference between being submissive and receptive. The truth is, men do like to be with intelligent or successful or pretty women—in part for their own ego, in part because they enjoy the dialogue or exchange—but they don't like to be with women who compete with or intimidate them. The problem of many single women caught in the grip of Androgynous Love is that because of their own "masculine identification," they are unwilling to accept male assertiveness in their dating partners. They want to dominate rather than submit. The opposite, of course, is also often the case, as many women look to being passively led rather than being an equal contributor, which places an impossible demand upon the man to deny his human vulnerability.

In a parallel fashion, many men complain that women want to be with a man who is more successful or aggressive or at least physically taller and that if you are at all a sensitive, vulnerable male, well, you are out of luck. But the fact is, women too want an equal partner: They want an emotionally sensitive partner but not a wimp. They want a man who talks like a woman but acts like a man. Yet many of the single men who struggle with Androgynous Love are female-identified and are therefore not interested in a sensitive, receptive dating partner—they want their date to initiate, lead, or dominate. In a way, they are looking for a woman who is more like a man. Of course, there is also the opposite Androgynous Love scenario with men as well. Many single men are so hypermasculine that they are looking for a date who is the sweet, admiring, unconditional yes-woman of yesterday.

So how do we get out of these fixed, polarized gender roles, either the traditional or the contemporary ones? Well, step by step . . .

STEP ONE: RECOGNIZING YOUR PATTERN

By now we know that in order to stop repeating a failed love pattern, we must first identify it and see it for what it is, which is often easier said than done. For example, a couple in their late thirties came to see me after dating seriously for a year, because they'd been unable to make a decision about their future. Given their age and their desire to have children, they felt it was time for them to either get married or call it quits. This is how the woman described the problem:

I really, truly love him, but I think we are just two different people. I always want to do things and go places and he doesn't. He likes the beach for vacation, but for me that's boring. I like skiing, the mountains, hiking, camping, or even traveling to Asia or Australia. He just likes to hang out. But it's not just about vacation. I like to plan things, and he is completely passive. He never takes the initiative. I'm ambitious about my career, but he's just happy coasting. Also, it bothers me that he is not assertive enough at work, like, he lets his boss mistreat him. When we first started going out I liked the fact that he was sensitive and nonaggressive, but now I wonder if we are just too different.

And this is how the boyfriend responded:

What she's saying is true. I have strong feelings for her as well, and I want to work it out, but I'm not sure it's possible. She's always on the go, always pushing to do things. And she doesn't really listen. And she is always on the computer or doing some work-related thing. I'm not as ambitious as she is and maybe I can't give her the lifestyle she wants, but I'm happy in my job. And I don't really want to go to all these places. I grew up in this area and I like to be close to my family. Her family is all over the place and she's not close to them, so she likes to travel. At the beginning of our relationship I liked her assertiveness and decisiveness, but now I see it more as insensitivity or pushiness or something. And it's really gotten worse since she was promoted to this management job a few months ago—she's become more bossy and aggressive.

As for many couples, it was difficult for this one to identify their Androgynous Love pattern for a couple of reasons. First and foremost, since their gender identifications were not along the obvious traditional definitions—she was more male-identified and he was more female-identified—they attributed their difficulties to personality rather than to gender differences. Consequently, and also because they were really at the beginning of their relationship, they concluded that the problem arose when they were getting to know each other and realizing that maybe they were just incompatible. Second, they attributed some of their difficulties to changing circumstances—her promotion at work "made her" more bossy or ambitious, further reinforcing the contrast or conflict between them. And finally, it struck them as politically incorrect or perhaps even reactionary to talk about important differences as a function of gender.

Now while there was an element of truth to the couple's understanding of the problem—as well as their resistance to stereotyping male and female differences—they had completely glossed over the critical role played by gender identification in their relationship. This is where careful history taking—in therapy as well as in your own implementation of Step One—comes in handy. Briefly, when I took a look at the woman's history, a clear, gender-related pattern emerged. The patient, Laura, would typically first get involved with a "nice," emotionally sensitive, and supportive man. But she would soon discover—or imagine—that this man was too needy, weak, or boring. Feeling he had no pizzazz, or was perhaps not successful enough, she would eventually break up with him. Then, attempting to learn from her mistake, she would try to date a more assertive, independent, or ambitious man. But here she would discover—or imagine—that this man was not treating her all that well. He is financially stable and responsible, she would think, but he is also insensitive, selfish, and critical. So she would break up with him too (or in a couple of instances would hang in there until he would break up with her).

Clearly, while her current relationship was longer and more serious than those other dating experiences, it definitely fit into a larger pattern. This pattern, with variations on the theme, is shared by many women. The order of the type of men dated might be reversed, or there might be a string of one type, followed by a string of the other. But basically, from the perspective of the archetypical contemporary single woman, the world of men seems to be divided into wimps and bullies. Now if you want to perpetuate this pattern, you hold on to the belief—articulated by many intelligent, perceptive women who share Laura's pattern—that men really do come in only these two varieties. To be fair, there is some truth to this perception, as in fact some men are more aggressive than others, and often enough nice guys are not sufficiently assertive or ambitious. But there is also the more balanced middle, where many successful *and* sensitive men reside in relative harmony. My patient Laura, however, could not see this center, because she herself was not in it.

This takes us into the work of Step Two, where you turn your attention from examining your partner to examining yourself. But before we go there, let's draw some of the red flags that could help you identify overly rigid gender identifications—traditional or reversed, in men and in women. This should get you out of the pattern of Androgynous Love before you're in it too deep. These red flags are sketched from a woman's perspective but as dictated by the logic of Androgynous Love, they apply equally as well to men. Consider, for example, Laura's boyfriend pattern, one that is shared by many contemporary men: he would get involved either with a self-confident, successful career woman whom he would then feel was too aggressive or with a sweet, supportive woman whom he would then perceive as lacking in independence, assertiveness, or intelligence. So for men, it's women who are either wimps or bullies.

Some Possible Markers of Wimps and Bullies

- He doesn't offer to treat you to dinner, doesn't call you for the second date, and doesn't have any preferences or suggestions as to what to do when you get together. (Wimp)

- He is not into his job and doesn't seem to have a plan for his future; he owes back taxes to the government and he says, "I don't really know what I want to do when I grow up." (Wimp)

- He is a nice, sensitive, and consistent guy, flexible and considerate to a fault. You feel you can get away with anything—he will always be there for you. The more bored you feel with him the needier he seems to become. He rather easily confesses to feeling insecure about you. (Wimp)

- He is always at work—even when he is with you (cell phone, BlackBerry, laptop). He expresses no emotions other than in bed, speaks like an automaton, and only wants to talk about politics, sports, cars, or business. He says women are neurotic or hysterical. (Bully)

- He is opinionated and argumentative, he insists that you have sex every time you get together, and he dismisses any talk about your relationship, your problems with your mother, or your work. (Bully)

- He tells you on your first date (or in his online dating profile) that he wants a woman who will let him go skiing or play golf with the guys, not bug him about drinking and watching football, and be a good mother and a decent cook. (Bully)

- He calls you after the first date to set up another, but he then cancels because of a last-minute work commitment, which then extends into two weeks during which he calls every other day to tell you he'd really like to see you as soon as his calendar clears up. He is not only driven by his work, but he seems to feel it's the center of the universe. (Bully)

STEP TWO: UNDERSTANDING YOUR AMBIVALENCE

Having identified and brought to a halt the pattern of Androgynous Love—where we are attracted to a stereotypically male or female quality in our date or partner and fall into a relationship with either a traditional or a reversed stereotyped, gender-based division of labor—we now must turn our focus away from our partner's rigid gender identification and onto ourselves. In Step Two your job is to *examine your own gender identification.*

Janice, a woman in her late thirties, came to see me after separating from her live-in boyfriend of seven years. A successful, senior fund manager in a Wall Street investment house, she came across as a highly competent, smart, and self-confident individual. She explained that she had been in a comfortable relationship that enabled her to pursue her career while having someone rooting for her and providing advice and support.

Unlike other men I dated, it didn't bother him, at least not in the beginning, that I was career-oriented, that I had my own opinions, and that I really wanted to create something and make money. And I liked the fact that he was not competing with me, not trying to put me in my place—believe me I get a lot of that from guys at work—and that he was a good listener and a truly kind man with good values. I liked the idea that we could one day really share being parents and I thought, and I still think, he would make a wonderful father. But after the first couple of years I started feeling he was too nice, you know what I mean, kind of mushy and not having a backbone. I felt he was wasting his time at work or even when he would take days off, he never did anything, just stay at home, drinking or watching TV or smoking dope. So I said something to him and then he

started complaining that I was too domineering and driven,
that I have wrong values, that I'm all about money, and not
enough about family and relationships.

This went on for a while and I kept thinking he'd change or
grow up. Finally, last year we went to a few sessions of couples
therapy, which made it even worse. I would tell him I needed
him to be more assertive and independent and he would say he
needed me to be more giving and supportive. But the more I
told him I wanted him to be strong, the weaker he would seem,
because he was just doing it for me. And the more he asked me to
be supportive, the wimpier he'd become, so the tougher and more
critical I became!

Like my patient Laura, Janice's relationship illustrated the
wisdom in the cliché about being careful of what you wish for.
She wished for a sensitive man and ended up with a wimp. Or
put another way, what she liked about her boyfriend at the out-
set was what she ended up hating later on. This symmetrical lack
of balance—going from one extreme to another—suggested to
Janice she was caught in a pattern; and because these extremes
had to do with what we typically think of as masculine and feminine traits, they suggested to her a gender-related pattern. Realizing this, Janice intuitively concluded, even before seeing me,
that if she simply left her boyfriend and replaced him with a
more aggressive, masculine man, she would end up with the
same problem, in reverse: wishing for a strong man, she would
find herself with a bully. So this was Janice's Step One, and it
brought her to couple's therapy, where she attempted to work on
her existing relationship.

Like many couples, however, in therapy Janice and her
boyfriend were unable to move beyond Step One, mostly because they insisted on correcting the imbalance in their gender
roles by *changing the other person*. But now, once the relationship

was over, and before getting into a new relationship, Janice was willing to move into Step Two. In turning the spotlight on her own gender identification, Janice remembered how as a young girl she consciously told herself she didn't want to be like her mother. The reason: her mother was financially and emotionally dependent on her husband. Even as a girl Janice perceived her mother as needy and weak and as victimized by her marriage. Her father she viewed as powerful, independent, and fun.

So over the years she again and again resolved to be independent, self-sufficient, and assertive, identifying, at least on the surface, with her father rather than her mother. And indeed, as an adult, her behaviors appeared more stereotypically masculine than feminine. As a result, when relating to men she was more like one of them: aggressive, active, ambitious, careless, and emotionally clueless. In a way she was fine with all this, the only problem being that these men did not want to date a competitor. They wanted to have at least the illusion of being in the driver's seat. They weren't going to passively follow her lead. So to get along with men romantically, Janice would have had to allow them to take the initiative. And she would have had to allow *herself* to receive their aggressive attention with passive receptivity. But this would have squarely placed her where she had vowed never to be—by her mother's side.

So that's how she ended up with a "wimp" who, because of his female identification, didn't require that she surrender her masculine identification. But ironically, the reason it ultimately didn't work out with this boyfriend was the same reason it couldn't have worked out with the bullies: she couldn't tolerate "weakness." In the case of the boyfriend, it was *his* weakness she had to get away from, and in the case of the bullies it was *her own* weakness she had to get away from. In both, this "weakness" was really no one's but her mother's. She couldn't be with the bullies because, with them, she would feel like her mother, and she couldn't be with the wimp because, with him, *he* would be like her mother. The bottom line: like all of us, she couldn't get away from her mother.

Now, even though as a child Janice consciously resolved to reject her mother's influence, she couldn't help but taking it in daily, absorbing and internalizing her mother's presence day in, day out. This was especially the case during her younger years when her mother was the primary caregiver and her father would spend most of his time at work or on the road. So while on the surface Janice was more like her father, deep inside, she was more like her mother—which is precisely why she was so terrified of that possibility. The psychological advantage of her seven-year relationship with the "wimp" was that it enabled her to project onto him the entire "wimp factor," so that she could continue to believe that she was nothing like her mother. But this failed because she couldn't tolerate that *he* was like her mother . . .

In sum, Step Two for Janice consisted of discovering that underneath her externally aggressive, masculine identification, she was nothing but a closeted wimp. Another way to put it is that because of her rejection of her mother as a role model, she was ambivalent about men—fearing her own "weakness," she couldn't accept their "strength" or masculinity. So she had opted for a man who was more feminine, with results that at least in psychological hindsight were all but predictable.

Now having finally realized that to a large extent her "wimps and bullies" construct was a projection of her own poorly integrated feminine and masculine sides, Janice for the first time felt free to focus on whether or not she liked the man she was dating *regardless* of his gender identification. Eventually Janice ended up with a man who was more on the bully side of the continuum. They had a good and lasting relationship, although one with plenty of conflict and some overt (not physical) aggression.

It was probably not ideal because it didn't reach the integration required by Step Three. But Janice was happier in this relationship than in her previous one.

Before discussing the integrative work of Step Three, let's pause here to review what you can do to evaluate your own mixed or conflicted gender identification. Once you "diagnose" yourself, you'll be ready for Step Three.

Diagnosing Your Own Conflicted Gender Identification

- Go back to pages 208–209 and check if any of the Bully or Wimp behaviors listed apply to you. Whether you are a man or a woman, that list describes the kind of rigid, polarized gender-based behavior that indicates a lack of male-female balance in one's identification.

- If you are a woman, look for the following constellation: You grew up with a mother who for some reason you couldn't respect. Either she was too dependent on your father or too needy of you. Perhaps she was too emotional, hysterical, or inarticulate. Maybe she was timid, fearful, and phobic. Perhaps she was just a stick-figure caricature of femininity. Recall if you have consistently dreaded ending up like your mother or have made a decision to not be like her in a significant way. Finally, examine whether on the surface you are more like your father—rational, aggressive, driven, detached, logical, or whatever the masculine similarity might be.

- If you are a man, look for the mirror-image constellation. You grew up with a father with whom, for one reason or another, you couldn't identify. Perhaps he was physically or emotionally absent; maybe he was intimidating, overpowering, or abusive; or maybe he was passive and withdrawn, leaving the entire field of influence to your mother. Now think of whether you have rejected your father as a model and took a page from your mother's book—are you more like her than him in sensitivity, need, passivity, or emotionality?

If you see yourself in one of these scenarios, join the club—it is one frequented by many in this postfeminist generation. It is also one of the most ubiquitous as well as overlooked psychological problems affecting romance. True, psychologists—academic and popular alike—still talk about the traditional form of male-female polarization and what to do about it. But not much is being said about the contemporary, more androgynous or reversed manifestation of the problem and how to resolve it.

STEP THREE: RESOLVING YOUR AMBIVALENCE

The good news is that the solution to the problem of Androgynous Love is there for the taking, right at the heart of the problem. In Step Three all you need to do is take the two ingredients we all have—masculinity and femininity—and reshuffle them until they reside together more harmoniously. It is no coincidence that our culture has often defined physical attractiveness in androgynous terms. Michelangelo's *David*, and even more so Donatello's sculpture of the same subject, are vivid and beautiful examples of the male and female forms blended into perfection. In more contemporary traditions, Mick Jagger, David Bowie, and Leonardo DiCaprio, to name just a few, are examples of androgynous men admired in adolescent culture. In one of literature's most famous celebrations of androgyny, Virginia Woolf described the moment in which her character, Orlando, magically transformed from a woman to a man, as follows: "The sound of the trumpets died away and Orlando stood stark naked. No human being, since the world began, has ever looked more ravishing. His form combined in one the strength of a man and a woman's grace." While this, indeed, is the physical or sexual ideal for many people, it is definitely the psychological ideal for most. One of the more common complaints of men in psychotherapy is that they are unable to cry or to be emotionally vulnerable. At the same time, they gripe that their girlfriends or spouses are too sensitive. Women in therapy often feel that they are too thin-skinned, while at the same time they complain that their male partners are emotionally oblivious. In other words, both genders would like to redistribute the male-female quotient in themselves, as well as in the other sex. In a very real sense, the contemporary, reversed form of Androgynous Love described in this chapter is the result of an unsuccessful attempt to do just that.

Because of this failure, some have suggested we return to the same rigid gender-based behaviors of the 1950s. But this, as I've shown, is just the flip side of the same problem. Therefore, I believe the quest for integrated androgyny—for both genders—is still the correct strategy. Our tactics, however, have to change. Whereas in the past women have attempted to correct an untenable or an inaccessible female gender identification by subsuming it under a more dominant male identification, they should now strive for a more or less equal integration of both. The same principle, of course, applies to men.

So if you are a forceful, take-charge, competitive, logical, type-A woman with no apparent signs of feminine softness, you need to get in touch with the sweet vulnerability you've repressed. Perhaps, as discussed above, you couldn't identify with a mother who was way too vulnerable, pathetically so, or maybe you grew up in a family of men and internalized their natural aggression as a defense against your more organic female sensitivity. Either way, if you want to be able to be more fully intimate with men, you must now reach for what you have repressed. As you probably know yourself, this repression is never successful anyway: I can hardly count the number of women I know—professionally and personally—who come across as male-identified barracudas, complete with an impressive portfolio of self-confidence, business savvy, and competitive edge but who end up experiencing and revealing their female vulnerability, sadly, by accepting poor treatment from would-be boyfriends or husbands for whose crumbs of love they masochistically and humiliatingly long.

If, on the other hand, you are a sweet, passive, receptive, and related woman with not an ounce of aggression, you need to bring forth some of the natural masculine aggression that surely lurks somewhere within. Perhaps you grew up with a career-obsessed, traveling, absent father, and a loving, available home-maker of a mother and therefore had no access to real-life male influence; or maybe you grew up in a family of girls with two older sisters and a sweet, passive father and therefore repressed any of your own aggression and masculine identification. Either way, if you wish to be able to relate to men, you must now reach for the male within. Of course, there could be many other reasons why you are afraid of being aggressive, assertive, or firm, but regardless, in all likelihood you've been exposed to and therefore have internalized masculine strength—if not from a father, brother, or grandfather, then from other masculine elements in the culture. So it's there, inside of you, and it now needs to come out.

THE DOER

Ellie was a rising, thirty-something-year-old corporate executive in a large consumer goods company. She came to see me with a clear agenda and purpose, a "mission statement" of sorts: "I've devoted my twenties to traveling and building my career and have been successful in both. But now I need to move on to the next stage in my life . . . to get married and have a family." Honest, straightforward, and practical, there was nevertheless a slightly annoying veneer to her introduction. Monitoring my own reaction to her presentation style, I asked about her history of dating and relationships.

It turned out that all of Ellie's relationships were with younger, sensitive men, some artistically inclined, others more spiritual or philosophical, but none who would match her in assertiveness, activity, or ambition. In each case she would fall in love with the softer, childlike, or dreamier aspect of the man's personality and would idealize it so that it took over all other aspects. In case after case, when the idealization waned, she would allow the other aspects to counterattack and eat away her love. In one relationship it upset her that the man had no potential for making money, in another that he smoked too much marijuana, and in a third that he had no understanding of the real world and wasn't at all a "doer."

Since she was eager to get results in therapy, in the best tradition of corporate project management, Ellie liked the idea of identifying patterns and following through with actionables. So we pretty quickly made it through Step One. Of course, in her case, it had only been wimps, which now helped me understand what was initially annoying about her presentation. Needing to be on top, in control, the initiator and the activator, Ellie left no room for me as a man to be anything but a wimp. Since it was not my natural tendency to be wimpy—especially not in my role as a therapist—I found her style a bit disconcerting. At this point I shared this observation with Ellie, and this ushered us into Step Two.

This was a more difficult terrain for Ellie, first because she had to let someone else (me) manage the therapeutic process, and second because she now had to get in touch with how much she was afraid of being like her mother, who, as it turned out, was extremely vulnerable and ineffectual. An unsuccessful artist, her mother "did nothing" with her life. As Ellie described it, she was a stay-at-home mom who would serve burned or under-cooked dinners along with rambling, emotional expressions of anxiety and self-doubt.

This, along with the subsequent realization that behind her fear of being like her mother was a wish to be just like her—the wish to not be in control but rather to be emotional, dependent, and needy, a natural childhood experience that was denied to her by the lack of a strong, reassuring mother—triggered in Ellie a significant amount of anxiety. After all, being assertive and ambitious, or male-identified, had worked for her so well in her career and was also all she had ever known. At the same time, this analysis appealed to her because in her mind we now identified the problem, which meant we were going to *do* something to fix it. Of course, this is where she had a real hard time because, at least in her case, Step Three involved not doing and fixing but rather the opposite: being and accepting. As we've seen throughout this book, Step Three always involves a process of integration. In the context of Androgynous Love this means integrating the wimp and the bully within, which for Ellie meant bringing forth her repressed feminine vulnerability—her hated but inescapable identification with her mother. But how do you do something like that? It's one thing to understand intellectually that if you become more feminine—emotional, vulnerable, sensitive, and receptive—you don't automatically become as ineffectual and as pathetic as you perceive your mother to have been. It's another thing to know what to actually *do* to make yourself more feminine.

Ellie, naturally, was a doer, so in trying to implement Step Three she embarked on a course of action to become more feminine. She structured time for herself to "work" on her feelings, took a course on "how to flirt," drew male-female diagrams with "pointers for moving forward," and scheduled "reciprocal feedback sessions" with friends, to help her stay on top of her progress. The paradox, of course, was that all this activity was pretty "masculine." It was a continuation of her defense against doing nothing and simply being, which she equated with her mother's incompetence, worthlessness, and emotional self-indulgence.

When I pointed that out to her, Ellie finally broke down and began to see that she couldn't be on top of it all. She gradually came to accept her limitations, frustrations, and helplessness, particularly in her inability to control her dating life and her relationships with men. Being herself, however, she continued to search for a concrete action, and she finally found one that made a big difference. Concluding that climbing the executive ladder in the "hierarchical, male-dominated culture" of her corporation had only reinforced her masculine identification, Ellie quit her job and took on a part-time consulting assignment, which gave her more time to hang out, reflect on her life, and "stay with her feelings." Of course, it also gave her more time to explore dating, and it came with a concomitant shift in her project management approach to dating. Contemplating for the first time that she might never find the right person and might never have a child, and allowing for her own despair, she made herself wholeheartedly available for dating, but for the first time she also stopped short of chasing men, giving them the opportunity to pursue her.

The self-help literature is full of advice for women like Ellie. "Don't call the guy—let him call you" is a common example of such tactical advice. But as a mere external behavior, this type of tactic won't work, because the only guy who would call is the "wimp" who is attracted to the bully in you. "Why wait for a call?" another book or therapist might say. "You should call him!" Well, this won't work either because the "bully" is not going to sit at home waiting for your call—he's out with the women he can bully. So these tactics will not work unless and until this type of woman becomes more interested in a partner with a better masculine-feminine balance. Happily, this is what happened to Ellie. When she ultimately met a man—also a consultant in her line of work—she allowed him to initiate and define their dating process. At the same time, she didn't freak out that he wasn't further along in his career and might never make huge amounts of money. He was not a perfect man, but he was both sweet and determined, and they were married within a year and had a child in two.

WINNING THE LOSER'S GAME

As we all know, being married is hardly a guarantee of a good enough relationship. And while there is no such guarantee, because of the universality and ever-present nature of the pattern of Androgynous Love—in its traditional or contemporary form—I believe that continuously working on Step Three will get you as close as possible to a guarantee. As we have seen before, trying to work on your relationship by asking or, worse, demanding your partner to change is a losing proposition. Much hostility in relationships is generated by the demand women make on men to "communicate," which really means, be more like a girlfriend and, likewise, by men's expectation that women "stop making a big deal out of everything," meaning, be more like a guy friend.

So instead of expecting your partner to work on integrating

his masculine-feminine split, put yourself in the hot seat and embrace the strategy of winning the loser's game. This strategy, discussed in a classic investment book bearing this title, was inspired by another book, about . . . tennis. In that book, the author, Simon Ramo, shows that while professional tennis players actually win their games, the winner in amateur games is determined by the actions of the loser, who basically defeats himself. Therefore, unless you are a pro, you can only win if you play not to lose, that is, if you play against yourself, not against your opponent.

When it comes to love, we are all amateurs, so in tennis terms rather than trying to smash the ball, we should try to just get it over the net. This, of course, requires that we stop second-guessing or trying to influence our opponent's—our game partner's—moves. As a first step, stop trying to beat some femininity (or masculinity) into your man, and accept his masculinity (or femininity) for what it is. This will free you to work on your own integration of grace and strength, feeling and thought, passivity and activity. It's only when you choose the road of integration—as long and slow as it may be—that somewhere along the path you'll notice that your partner is now on a parallel road. Although you didn't try to influence him, you probably did anyway, both by modeling, and by freeing him from the previous, polarizing dynamic, in which you had seized all the feminine (or masculine) territory and that had therefore left for him only the opposite terrain. Now that you are no longer the emotional wreck, he doesn't have to be the calm and composed thinker. Or now that you are no longer the driven workaholic, he doesn't have to be the one worrying about your relationship and the children—he can focus on his own career.

As we saw in Ellie's case above, when truly out of balance, recalibrating your masculine-feminine identification is a tall order. It means going beyond the either-or orientation of Step Two in which you compromise, figuring that because you are a bully, you have to live with your ambivalence about your wimpy partner (or vice versa). It means going for the whole thing, for the best thing, for having it all—the bully *and* the wimp—in yourself and in your partner. It therefore involves doing some new, unfamiliar things or *not* doing some highly habituated things. This is difficult to describe in practical terms without resorting to gender-based clichés and without losing sight of the many individual variations. After all, what's masculine for one person might be feminine for another, in part because it depends not only on the activity in question but also on how you do it. Finally, while we all have both feminine and masculine traits, we can never achieve, nor should we aspire to achieve, a perfect balance. Although psychologically speaking, men and women are fundamentally more alike than different, there will always be psychological differences between the sexes, as well as a subjective sense of being different. So whereas integration is a worthy goal, we must never believe that we can completely transcend our own gender.

Having said that, let's visit some of the possible concrete behaviors that, when taken as part of an underlying strategy to integrate your internal gender identifications, can help you achieve greater balance. To start with, undertaking psychotherapy is probably the single best thing you can do, because by its very nature, psychotherapy combines and facilitates both an internal process and an external, behavioral change. Short of that, changing some of your external behaviors in the tradition of "fake it till you make it" will help you to develop an internal shift as well.

Women who tend to be more male-identified can work on deepening their relationship with their mother. Paradoxically, this may well mean learning from some of their mother's more so-called superficial achievements. Recalling that these women have often rejected their mothers in childhood because they couldn't look up to them explains this paradox. If your mother tends to be overly emotional, reactive, hysterical, needy, and so on, it's understandable that you couldn't have—and perhaps still can't have—a deep relationship with her, one that would facilitate a healthy female identification. But over the years you've probably thrown out the baby with the bath water: surely your mother has some redeeming "feminine" features, superficial as they may seem. She might be into clothing and have great taste or a facility with makeup; or maybe she knows how to flirt; or maybe she's creative, can decorate, or can be playful; or maybe the upside of being hysterical is the ease of really feeling and of expressing those feelings. So perhaps you can now engage with your mother around any of these—for example, let her take you shopping for clothes or jewelry. The idea is that with time you will begin to reidentify with some of your mother's feminine attributes that you have previously shunned.

In addition, developing close relationships with other women, especially those who have a better balance in their own gender identification, can be of help. And along these lines, stay away from women who are too much like your mother or those who have given up on men altogether by, psychologically speaking, becoming one themselves. Finally, learning to enjoy some small, insignificant, gender-based behaviors practiced by women for generations, such as shopping, putting on makeup, getting a manicure, sharing recipes, knitting, and talking about relationships, can help you to appreciate and reclaim some of your lost or hidden femininity. If you go down this road, however, do it in your own time and style, and try to choose behaviors that work for *you*, not for your mother, boyfriend, or husband.

In sum, for the male-identified woman, the central strategy is to seek positive female influences. Clearly, the same concept applies in principle to the traditional, hypermasculine male, who would do well to reach out for feminine influence in order to soften up his aggressive exterior and draw out the girl within (he too grew up with a mother or other feminine influences). Of course, it's unlikely he'd take up knitting or makeup, but he might well find his own way into discussing relationships, cooking, gardening, or other, historically feminine preoccupations. Similarly, the traditional, hyperfeminine woman can expand her horizons by reading about money, politics, or sports, and by resting some of her self-esteem on such concrete, male-oriented achievements as getting a raise at work, fixing the garage door, and driving aggressively (without getting a ticket). Finally, given the logic of Androgynous Love, the more contemporary, female-identified man would do well to follow the same path, seeking in adulthood the kind of positive male influences he most likely didn't have as a child.

In a famous Renaissance painting, the artist Titian captured a universal moment in the war between the sexes: the goddess Venus is trying to hold on to her lover, Adonis, so as to prevent him from going off to the hunt. Painted as a large, naked, literally grounded woman, Venus is seen imploring and restraining a strong, impatient, adolescent-looking Adonis, who is being pulled away by three dogs geared up for the hunt. Amazingly, notwithstanding the tremendous social changes of the second half of the twentieth century, this traditional gender-based dynamic is well and alive. Although men no longer go hunting while women cook, it will take evolution millions of years to reprogram the DNA of our gender identity. For better or worse, this gender identity is part of our biological and psychological heritage. Ignoring this has led us to the contemporary version of Androgynous Love, in which gender roles are indeed reversed, but neither women nor men are any happier. Accepting it as a starting point, on the other hand, will enable us to feel more secure in our primary gender identification and therefore more open to the balancing influences of the opposite sex.

When Love Goes Right

I think I'm getting the hang of it," the patient smiled as she was telling me about her new relationship. "Maybe you are," I said. "Maybe her problem is not as big as I thought," I said to myself. "Maybe sometimes love is simple." But a couple of months later this compelling thirty-something professional decided that this was not the man of her dreams after all. So she broke up the relationship and once again found herself in the same state of disillusionment and apprehension or, to use the clinical terms, depression and anxiety, that brought her into my office a year earlier. Her previously expressed hope, which now turned out to be more of a denial, was merely part of her long-standing, failed relationship pattern.

Like most great ideas, love, in theory, is simple. In reality, however, it is quite complicated, because, as I've tried to show in this book, it can never be free of ambivalence. While ambivalence is still a relatively simple concept, our attempt to deny it drives us into the self-deluded patterns of failed love, which is where things get complicated. In striving for simplicity, I separated these patterns into seven separate chapters, each opening with an interpretative illustration from Greek mythology. These ancient myths, I should note, mirror life in their simplicity as well as complexity. For example, in the story of Apollo and Daphne, in which the former chases the latter and catches her only to feel her fading heartbeat as she turns into a laurel tree in his arms, the pain of One-Way Love is beautifully and simply portrayed. But the story also has a clear narcissistic twist, for as Ovid tells us, Apollo, after capturing the nymph, exclaimed, "Since you can never be my bride, / My tree at least you shall be!" And he then declared that from that day on all Roman war heroes would wear a laurel wreath to symbolize triumph. In reality too, when we pursue unavailable people it is often an indication not only of One-Way Love, but also of Narcissistic Love: we are drawn to the unavailable person not only as a means of avoiding ambivalence by longing for what we can't have but also because we hope to elevate our low self-esteem with the prospect of conquest or acceptance. So as I've said before, the seven patterns of failed love are interrelated, which is why the three-step approach to overcoming them, described in each chapter, is underlined by the same process.

As happens in psychotherapy, in attempting to "diagnose" and "cure" relationships, this book has likely highlighted the negatives, drawing perhaps a slightly distorted view of love. The French analyst Jacques Lacan took this to a poetic, if cynical, extreme, concluding that "love is giving something you don't have to someone you don't know." While Lacan may have captured an aspect of romantic love, as a more optimistic antidote I'd like to suggest the poetics of Rainer Maria Rilke. In a letter about love, Rilke wrote that young people "must not forget, when they love, that they are beginners, bunglers of life, apprentices in love,— must *learn* love." Stipulating, from my clinical experience, that when it comes to love we are all young, I particularly like Rilke's explanation, especially coming as it is from such as passionate, sensual, and romantic poet:

> Like so much else, people have also misunderstood the place of love in life, they have made it into play and pleasure because they thought that play and pleasure were more

blissful than work; but there is nothing happier than work, and love, just because it is the extreme happiness, can be nothing else but work.—So whoever loves must try to act as if he had a great work: he must be much alone and go into himself and collect himself and hold fast to himself; he must work; he must become something!

So yes, we must work—and we'd better enjoy this work—if we are to overcome Lacan's darker vision of love. One of my patients once observed, "This is all about work, patterns, defenses, issues . . . What does a good relationship look like?" It is indeed difficult to draw a picture of healthy, mature love, not only for the psychologist, who by virtue of his work deals more with the dilemmas than the delights of love, but also for the novelist. Great works of literature from all cultures are full of tragic, tormented, "pathological" love stories. A good relationship is clearly less dramatic than a turbulent one and, in that respect, perhaps even somewhat boring. Nonetheless, my patient said it would be helpful to draw such a picture, so in concluding, I'd like to offer my top ten (actually twelve) must-haves in a good-enough relationship. Presumably, if you go through the three-step approach offered in this book, including, most particularly, the integrative work of Step Three, you'll end up with a long-term relationship that will have most if not all of the following qualities:

• *A certain degree of mutual idealization.* Too much of it, and we are in the territory of Narcissistic Love, but too little means there's nothing special about our relationship. In a long-term relationship, idealization can wax and wane, but it must always be there in potential, ready to rekindle the flame when necessary.
• *A deep identification with each other.* The ability to relate to something fundamental in the other person's life experience. This can originate from having experienced a similar trauma in

childhood, having grown up in a similar family dynamic, or from anything else that would resonate deeply within each other's psyche. This is what makes you feel your partner is your soul mate.

• *A balance of similarities and opposites in personality.* A basic similarity or compatibility in philosophy of life, values, and sensibilities is essential, but too much sameness is boring; it presents no opportunity to learn to love outside of oneself. Opposites do attract and can be complimentary, which makes for a great partnership, but too much or too many of them can lead to polarization, discord, and alienation.

• *The ability to talk.* Communicating implies talking about the important feelings, thoughts, and decisions that affect the couple's life. This is critical, but so is engaging in pleasurable small talk and in conversations about "external subject matters" such as politics or food or art or sports or psychology or whatever.

• *Sex.* When it comes to love relationships, sex—expanded to include the dynamics of attraction, affection, and courting—is what makes the world go round. Perhaps even more so than money. While in a long-term relationship sexual desire and excitement tend to decrease with time, and frequency of sex might decrease even more, we can't quite speak of romantic love without a sexual component. Indeed, for many couples, a relationship without sex feels like a death sentence.

• *Tolerating and resolving conflict.* It's not always easy to communicate loving, warm and fuzzy feelings, but it's even harder to express such negative feelings as anger and disappointment. Yet the ability to deal with conflict directly—by airing out negative feelings—as well as the know-how and willingness to resolve it and move on until next time, are critical.

• *Implicit or explicit ground rules.* Fights are unavoidable and can also be constructive in facilitating change or in pointing out important differences in priorities and needs. Other upsets, grievances, and misunderstandings are also inescapable. But even in hard times there has to be a mutual agreement—spoken or understood—that certain behaviors are basically out of bounds. The specifics of these behaviors vary from couple to couple but often include such transgressions as verbal abuse, extramarital sex, and physical violence.

• *Affect and impulse regulation.* Related to the previous two points, both individuals must have the basic capacity to contain their feelings and to refrain from acting on impulse. If one of the partners slips and acts out (e.g., sexually or in anger), the other must be able to keep his reaction in check so as to prevent reciprocal escalation.

• *Individual capacity for self-reinvention.* In truly long-term relationships each partner must have enough self-love and drive to be committed to his own growth, so that he doesn't end up existing as a satellite revolving around the other partner. In addition to minimizing unhealthy dependency, this makes it possible for you to periodically reinvent yourself—an essential coping strategy for dealing with life's inevitable changes, crises, and stresses, which can damage even a good-enough relationship.

• *A joint generative project greater than the self.* Most commonly this means having children, but it doesn't have to. The essential feature here is that in a "lifelong" relationship, the couple should have a significant joint involvement in something other than themselves. This could be a commitment to a political cause, community work, or animals. Without this there is too much "narcissistic pressure" on the relationship—too much demand for endless joy and pleasure from each other, which no relationship can sustain in the long run.

• *An unquestioned internal personal belief in the value of commitment.* This carries you through hard times and gives you the motivation to work on the relationship. Both partners need to share this belief, for without it, there's little reason not to look for a better relationship every few years.

• And last . . . *in love as in life, a bit of magic, unaccounted for by psychology, and some good fortune, unearned by hard work, can make a big difference.*

BIBLIOGRAPHY

Angrist, S. W. 1998, December 24. "Business Bookshelf: It Doesn't Grow on Trees." *Wall Street Journal*, p. A7.

Becker, E. 1997. *The Denial of Death*. New York: The Free Press.

Bollas, C. 1987. *The Shadow of the Object, Psychoanalysis of the Unthought Known*. New York: Columbia University Press.

———. 1991. *Forces of Destiny*. London: Free Association Books.

Brandes, S. 1980. *Metaphors of Masculinity*. Philadelphia: University of Pennsylvania Press.

Donington, R. 1963. *Wagner's "Ring" and Its Symbols*. London: Faber Paperbacks.

Ellis, C. D. 1998. *Winning the Loser's Game: Timeless Strategies of Successful Investing*. New York: McGraw-Hill.

Erikson, E. 1950. *Childhood and Society*. New York: W. W. Norton.

Fairbairn, W. R. D. 1952. *An Object-Relations Theory of the Personality*. New York: Basic Books.

Fogel, G. I., Lane, F. M., and Liebert, R. S., eds. *The Psychology of Men*. New Haven, CT: Yale University Press.

Freud, S. 1900. *The Interpretation of Dreams*. In James Strachney, ed., *The Standard Edition of the Complete Psychological Works of Sigmund Freud* (Vols. 4–5). London: Hogarth Press, 1958.

———. 1905. *Three Essays on the Theory of Sexuality*. In James Strachey, ed., *The Standard Edition of the Complete Psychological Works of Sigmund Freud* (Vol. 7, pp. 125–245). London: Hogarth Press, 1964.

————. 1915. *Instincts and their Vicissitudes.* In James Strachey, ed., *The Standard Edition of the Complete Psychological Works of Sigmund Freud* (Vol. 14, pp. 117–40). London: Hogarth Press, 1957.

————. 1917. *Mourning and Melancholia.* In James Strachey, ed., *The Standard Edition of the Complete Psychological Works of Sigmund Freud* (Vol. 14, pp. 237–60). London: Hogarth Press, 1957.

————. 1920. *Beyond the Pleasure Principle.* In James Strachey, ed., *The Standard Edition of the Complete Psychological Works of Sigmund Freud* (Vol. 18, pp. 3–64). London: Hogarth Press, 1955.

————. 1924. *The Economic Problem of Masochism.* In James Strachey, ed., *The Standard Edition of the Complete Psychological Works of Sigmund Freud* (Vol. 19, pp. 155–70). London: Hogarth Press, 1961.

————. 1926 *Inhibitions, Symptoms and Anxiety.* In James Strachey, ed., *The Standard Edition of the Complete Psychological Works of Sigmund Freud* (Vol. 20, pp. 70–175). London: Hogarth Press, 1968.

————. 1933. *New Introductory Lectures on Psycho-Analysis.* In James Strachey, ed., *The Standard Edition of the Complete Psychological Works of Sigmund Freud* (Vol. 22, pp. 1–182). London: Hogarth Press.

Gay, P. 1988. *Freud: A Life for Our Time.* New York: W. W. Norton.

Gaylin, W., and Person, E., eds. 1988. *Passionate Attachments: Thinking About Love.* New York: The Free Press.

Grant, M. 1995. *Myths of the Greeks and Romans.* New York: Meridian.

Gratch, A., 2002. *If Men Could Talk: Translating the Secret Language of Men.* New York: Little, Brown.